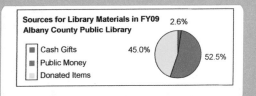

Sources for Library Materials in FY09
Albany County Public Library

- Cash Gifts
- Public Money
- Donated Items

2.6%
45.0%
52.5%

LEILA GROSSMAN/GRANNIS PHOTOGRAPHY

Anna Jane Grossman is a New York-based freelance writer specializing in lifestyle and arts and entertainment features. Her work has appeared in dozens of publications, including the *New York Times*, Salon.com, the *Washington Post*, the Associated Press, *Elle*, *New York Magazine*, *Marie Claire*, and *Fortune*.

For more information, visit annajane.net

OBSOLETE

andlines * Privacy * Camera Film * Getting Lost * Encyclopedias
hone Sex * Writing Letters * Licking Stamps * Hitchhikers * Boo
olodexes * Landlines * Passbooks * Camera Film * Photo Albums *
ex * Tokens * Hitchhikers * Boom Boxes * Cursive Writing * Encyc
olodexes * Landlines * Pay Phones * Tonsillectomies * Getting L
ruly Blind Dates * Phone Sex * Laugh Tracks * Late Fees * House
anual Car Windows * Rolodexes * Long-Distance Charges * Pennie
ncyclopedias * Mixtapes * Truly Blind Dates * Phone Sex * Writi
itchhikers * Asbestos * Cursive Writing * Manual Car Windows *
raditional Names * Getting Lost * Encyclopedias * Mixtapes * Tr
hite Pages * Hitchhikers * Boom Boxes * Cursive Writing * Canne
anual Car Windows * Rolodexes * Milkmen * Percolators * Travele
hones * Encyclopedias * Betamax * Truly Blind Dates * Phone Sex
ackaging * Boom Boxes * Cursive Writing * Manual Car Windows *
iss (and Mrs.) * Privacy * Camera Film * Pocket Protectors * En
apes * Audiotapes * Camcorders * Writing Letters * Unflattering
lothes * Hitchhikers * Ditto Paper * Cursive Writing * Super 8s
anual Car Windows * Rolodexes * Airport Good-byes * Plastic Ba
ube Television Sets * Getting Lost * Encyclopedias * Mixtapes *
hone Sex * Writing Letters * Licking Stamps * AM Radio * Boom B
riting * Rolodexes * Maps * Singles Bars * Camera Film * Pornogr
ncyclopedias * Mixtapes * Truly Blind Dates * Phone Sex * Writi
icking Stamps * Hitchhikers * Boom Boxes * Answering Machines *
icrofilm/Microfiche * Analog Clocks * Typewriters * Sadness * E
ixtapes * Appendicitis Scars * Dial-up Modems * Writing Letter
itchhikers * Boom Boxes * Canned Laughter * Rolodexes * Anonymi
ald Spots * Truly Blind Dates * Books * Writing Letters * Licki
rcades * Buffering * Cursive Writing * MSG * Rolodexes * Layaway
hort Basketball Shorts * Encyclopedias * Mixtapes * Doing Noth
inidiscs * Licking Stamps * Hitchhikers * Boom Boxes * Cursive W
arm Studs * Landlines * Newspapers * Underscore/Underline * Sho
ixtapes * Lighthouses * Phone Sex * Writing Letters * Checks * H
ursive Writing * Manual Car Windows * Rolodexes * Landlines * S
etting Lost * Encyclopedias * Capitalization * Truly Blind Dat
riting Letters * CDs * Hitchhikers * Boom Boxes * Cursive Writi
olodexes * Dying of Old Age * Niche Publications * Car Cigaret
aper Plane Tickets * Writing Letters * Hitchhikers * Cash * Cur
orrection Fluid * Rolodexes * Landlines * Skate Keys * Mail * Ge
ixtapes * Truly Blind Dates * Phone Sex * Writing Letters * Lic
oom Boxes * Cursive Writing * Manual Car Windows * Rolodexes * L
etting Lost * Encyclopedias * Mixtapes * Truly Blind Dates * Ph
icking Stamps * Hitchhikers * Boom Boxes * Cursive Writing * Ma
olodexes * Landlines * Privacy * Camera Film * Getting Lost * Enc
ruly Blind Dates * Phone Sex * Writing Letters * Licking Stamp

pes * Truly Blind Dates
* Cursive Writing * Manual Car Windows
eys * Mixtapes * Blackboards * Phone
s * Phone Sex
ult Book Stores * Mixtapes
Boom Boxes * Cursive Writing
Economics * Plaster Casts
ers * After-School Specials
eetings * Body Hair
nd Dates * Phone Sex
ter
cks * Rotar

OBSOLETE

AN ENCYCLOPEDIA OF ONCE-COMMON THINGS PASSING US BY

eating
ursive
agazines
ers
s * Rolodexes
edias
eos
yclopedias
ps
t * Camera Film
Work * Comb-overs
* Manual Car Windows
* Encyclopedias
ers * Boom Boxes
s * Camera Film
ne Sex * AM Radio
ning Socks
hters
riting * Girdles
ost * Encyclopedias
tamps * Hitchhikers
s * Privacy * Push-Buttons
x * Writing Letters
ar Windows
dias * Mixtapes
hhikers * Boom Boxes

ANNA JANE GROSSMAN

ILLUSTRATIONS BY JAMES GULLIVER HANCOCK

**ABRAMS IMAGE
NEW YORK**

Editor: David Cashion
Designer: Alissa Faden
Production Manager: Jacqueline Poirier

Library of Congress Cataloging-in-Publication Data
Grossman, Anna Jane.
 Obsolete : an encyclopedia of once-common things passing us by / by Anna
Jane Grossman ; illustrated by James Gulliver Hancock.
      p. cm.
 ISBN 978-0-8109-7849-2 (Harry N. Abrams, Inc.)
1. Material culture—United States—Encyclopedias. 2. Product
obsolescence—United States—Encyclopedias. 3. Technology—United
States—Encyclopedias. 4. Popular culture—United States—Encyclopedias. 5.
Social change—United States—Encyclopedias. 6. United States—Social life
and customs—Encyclopedias. 7. United States—Civilization—Encyclopedias.
I. Hancock, James Gulliver. II. Title.
E161.G77 2009
306.4 60973—dc22

                         2009008155

Printed and bound in China
10 9 8 7 6 5 4 3 2 1

Abrams Image books are available at special discounts when purchased in quantity for
premiums and promotions as well as fundraising or educational use. Special editions can
also be created to specification. For details, contact specialmarkets@abramsbooks.com or the
address below.

THE ART OF BOOKS SINCE 1949

115 West 18th Street
New York, NY 10011
www.abrams.com

CONTENTS

INTRODUCTION

When I was in high school, I met Beatrice, a reclusive eighty-five-year-old who lived on Manhattan's Lower East Side. She and I started having breakfast every Wednesday. We'd drink coffee and sample the offerings from the artisanal donut shop downstairs from her apartment, located in a former bialy factory. I had moments where I hoped she'd let loose a font of profundity that would change my life and inspire some kind of *Tuesdays with Morrie* oeuvre, but she wasn't that kind of old lady: Her three favorite words were "I'm a bitch." Ornery as she was, I kept it up for a decade—they were amazing donuts.

I think I was a kind of enigma to Beatrice—a visitor from a world that had changed a great deal since she'd played an active part in it. The idea that I was able to work from home via computer after college was something she never could grasp. She was flummoxed by the way I carried a tiny phone, but often didn't pick it up when it rang. Whenever she left me a voicemail, she slowly spelled out her full name as if dictating a formal telegram.

There were many aspects of her life that I found inscrutable as well. At her bank, she knew the manager by name; I hadn't been past my branch's ATM vestibule since I'd opened an account. When I replaced her broken rotary phone with a touchtone one, she had to memorize where each number was located—she'd never seen a phone with buttons, and the digits were too small for her to read. And yet there were many banal tasks that she could do that I probably never will: light an oven's pilot light without flinching, make coffee in a percolator, mend a bra, or balance a checkbook by hand. In some ways, our lives were parallel: She too had been a single career woman living in Brooklyn, but back then, that meant something. When she opened an electrolysis office on Fourteenth Street in the 1940s, her brother had to sign the lease because the landlord wouldn't rent to a single woman. We both loved traveling, but I did it mostly by car and plane, while she'd largely used trains. She loved to face backward in the dining car, where she'd smoke cigarettes while flipping through *Reader's Digest.*

When Beatrice passed away at ninety-five, some of her belongings dribbled into my apartment. My seven-year-old niece was fascinated by Beatrice's rotary phone, her shoehorn, a small pile of carbon paper—all things she'd never seen before. She even marveled over a plain plastic flashlight that had a simple white switch and faint yellowy light. I teased her: "You've never seen a flashlight?" She got one off of a key chain on her backpack. "They're supposed to be like this," she said. The tiny thing lit up, three miniscule LED lights sending an impossibly bright bluish-white beam across the room.

The objects that most interested me were actually the ones I'd bought for Beatrice in the late 90s: The touchtone phone already looked clunky, with its thick antenna and built in cassette-tape answering machine. The address book that I'd helped her fill out, its pages now yellowing, reminded me that it had been years since I'd added a new name to my Rolodex. When I had started seeing her, I was someone who carried a Filofax at all times and had a pager. I got an e-mail account in the 11th grade, but I shared it with the sixty other kids in my class—if I recall correctly, the address was 00111.8347@compuserve.com.

So many of the changes that took place during the ten years that I knew Beatrice were rooted in technology, but most of them had affected me in ways far beyond anything that lived as pixels on a screen. In the interim years, I'd become someone who regularly used the Internet to share intimate details about my life on something that I first knew as a "b-log." It seems like I have a new cell phone every year, and, thanks to speed dial, I've never learned my boyfriend's number. I have little doubt that my iPod will need to be replaced before I finish this paragraph. And yet, it wasn't really so long ago that I knew every button and curve and scratch on my yellow and gray Sony Sports Walkman AM/FM cassette player (the one with the clip and rubber buttons), or that I kept a leather-bound diary, or could dial my friends with my eyes closed. When the phone rang, I said "Hello?" The question mark was there because I didn't know who was calling.

What happened to that person? And what will happen to all the Sony Sports being offered up as $40 "vintage" items on eBay? Perhaps I'll tell my children how I used to have to Rollerblade five blocks in the rain in order to purchase CDs. Or maybe I'll amaze them with stories about sending text messages and getting Netflix and driving in hybrid cars.

Of course, one expects an older generation to wax poetic about how they grew up in simpler times, but the world really *was* a less complicated place last year, last decade, last century. Computing hardware is the best example of this trend. In 1965, Intel's cofounder, Gordon Moore, predicted that the number of transistors that could be put on a chip would double every two years. The idea, which came to be known as Moore's Law, was right on the money. It's the principle that has brought us gadgets that are constantly increasing in ability as they shrink in size. But are smaller computers making us happier? Is the playlist I made for the gym last night really giving me that much more joy than the homemade mixtapes I used to listen to? It's hard to say, but I do think it's given me an increased awareness of the ephemeral nature of all the everyday things that are passing by faster than ever before. It's imbued me with a kind of odd nostalgia for *right now*.

Perhaps that's just the price to pay for living in a world that can't seem to shift out of fifth gear. In 1970, the futurist Alvin Toffler wrote *Future Shock*, a book in which he posited that the rate of change in the world was drastically accelerating, and that physical and psychological overload would likely occur. If progress is happening exponentially, the pace at which things become obsolete seems to be close to hitting terminal velocity. Today, we experience in one year the amount of change that it would've taken generations to experience a few hundred years ago. I have little doubt that the world Beatrice was born into was more similar to the one her great-grandparents lived in than my world was to hers.

"When we lived in an agrarian world as peasants, life was set by the seasons and things were slow. Terribly slow. You had the same plot of land your whole life. Nothing much happened within your lifetime," Mr. Toffler said when I was able to use the Web to track down his office number (something that would've been next to impossible before Google—hey, sometimes progress really is progress). "Today, people are running faster and harder and are having difficulty keeping up with the pace of life." Schools, he says, are an example of how hard it is to operate at the current pace of change. He argues that even the most forward-thinking institutions are doling out educations that won't be applicable to tomorrow's world. "We are essentially preparing kids for tasks they won't need and jobs that won't exist." In terms of schools teaching essential life skills, I agree with him. While some of the more practical things I learned in high school have proven to be quite useful—typing and driving for example—I learned nothing that prepared me to write e-mails or use Google or do the kind of telecommuting I do and have the discipline to make my own schedule. All those hours I spent practicing cursive writing or figuring out programming in BASIC or learning how to use card catalogs and microfiche . . . I don't regret learning those things, but they are skills that are even less useful than the stuff I *knew* wasn't going to be relevant to my life (ahem, calculus).

The question is: What happens to bits of knowledge that are no longer relevant? Some of it, I imagine, will be handed down, at least for another couple of centuries—I've seen academic journals with articles on, say, mid-eighteenth-century butter dishes, and there are still people out there who make chainmail suits. I like to think that one day someone who has yet to be born will while away years learning all there is to know about our era's pay phones or printed dictionaries or manual car windows. But there likely won't be: The more advances we make, the more slips away. In his 1993 book, *Beginning Again*, the biologist David Ehrenfeld uses the example of earthworms: At the time he was writing, European and Asian earthworms were displacing native ones in America and the ecologic consequences were potentially quite great. But Mr. Ehrenfeld found that there was only one single US scientist left who had studied earthworm taxonomy (Australia and England had none). With so many other exciting branches of science materializing and getting funding and attracting scholars, even the most basic knowledge about earthworms was being completely lost. There was a similar problem when a turret on the battleship *Iowa* blew up in 1989, he notes. The ship was from World War II, and both the materials and the technical knowledge necessary to repair it no longer existed. "Most of us probably imagine knowledge to be cumulative: Each advance is built on prior discoveries, block piled upon block in an ever-growing edifice," Mr. Ehrenfeld writes. "We don't think of the blocks underneath as crumbling away or, worse yet, simply vanishing."

This book is an attempt to take stock of things in our lives that are hanging on by threads: ideas, habits, and objects that are either obsolete or well on their way. It's easy to confuse obsolescence with things just going out of style, but I've done my best to distinguish between those two categories. Fads come and go, but something begins to seem obsolete when it is no longer in use, either because it's been supplanted by something that's perceived as categorically better or faster or stronger or easier, or because the purpose it served has exited stage right. It's not an exact science, but I would argue that A-frame houses, variety shows, and top hats may one day cycle back into style; typewriters, traveler's checks, and VCRs probably won't. I've largely tried not to use brand names, since those tend to be fungible; I have made a handful of exceptions for products, like the Polaroid and the Rolodex, which were such titans that calling them anything else would be reductive. Plenty of things I've covered are still very much a part of our lives, but may not be for long. Other subjects are pretty well in our past, but I've included them because they are still within the reach of our collective conscious.

There are many staunch defenders of sundry objects that are obsolete (or on the brink), and I was lucky enough to talk to some of them while researching the pieces in this collection. Scholars studying antique mercury thermometers in the year 3084 will owe a lot to Richard Porter, an eighty-year-old former science teacher who has spent twenty years manning his Thermometer Museum in Onset, Massachusetts, filled with more than a thousand kinds of thermometers. (Penn State is currently in the process of making an inventory of his collection, which it plans to absorb into a new weather museum.) Craig Poirier, an AM stereo enthusiast in Nova Scotia, gave me a complete education about the low-frequency stations he loves and has watched—or heard—die out: This year, the last of Halifax's AM stations turned off its signal. I spoke to Mike Smith of Mission Viejo, California, a former milkman who started leaving bottles on doorsteps when he was just eight years old and is now working to document the history of dairy delivery in Southern California. Then there was the inimitable Matt "Tapes" Steck, a valiant defender of analog media, despite the fact that he is only twenty. Look for him if you're ever in Douglasville, Pennsylvania—he's the guy walking around with one of his twenty-odd boom boxes lovingly balanced on his shoulder. I also had the privilege of talking to several twentieth-century luminaries—from Madeleine Albright to Larry Flynt—about how they've been affected by the acceleration of progress.

It would be impossible to write a fully comprehensive book on something as omnipresent as obsolescence, but my hope is that the following pages serve as a kind of time capsule that might help us to take stock of the world we're in right now through the lens of the one we're leaving behind. My goal has been neither to preach the sanctity of time gone by, nor to lament the steady hum of progress. We're all on this train together, and it only moves in one direction. Still, it's nice sometimes to sit backward and be reminded of where we've been.

ADULT BOOK STORES

A place outside of the home to privately indulge prurient interests that had nothing to do with reading.

AFTER-SCHOOL SPECIALS

Didactic television dramas aimed at youths, broadcast in the afternoons by ABC from the 1970s through the 90s; preached the dangers of teen pregnancy, drugs, hitchhiking, (see page 86) and bowl cuts. The term came to refer to any kind of televised morality play aimed at teens.

AGING

A biological process that occurred before the advent of plastic surgery. Signs of aging (or, speaking euphemistically, "maturing") often included graying hair, increased wrinkles, varicose veins, a lessening of shame, a desire to move to Arizona, and sometimes the proclivity to relieve oneself in public. Non-physical signs of aging may still be observed, such as (but not limited to) the desire to buy hot pants, drive a Ferrari, or play slot machines.

AIRPORT GOOD-BYES

The practice of accompanying someone (often a dewy-eyed lover) all the way to the gate at the airport, now thought to be as potentially dangerous as a handbag containing Scope; currently only possible with the purchase of an additional ticket.

AM RADIO

Radio channels that operated in the relatively low 500–to 1,600-kilo-hertz range; home of the Packers and Rush Limbaugh, I-95, and Jesus.

·　·　·

AM stations, if you can tune them in at all, are so often realms of pon-tificating jockeys, bummer health news, and scintillating traffic analysis that it's easy for many of us to just completely ignore that entire spec-trum of the dial. Not long ago, however, AM—short for amplitude modulation—was the only option for radio users.

For the bulk of its ninety-plus-year lifetime, the AM dial played mostly music and had a kind of magic ability to span great distances. While its ground-wave signal only reached locally during the day, at night it would bounce off the atmosphere and the water, enabling it to travel thousands of miles. This meant that the strongest signals gave people glimpses of lives in parts of the country they might never see. *Grand Ole Opry*, which, as of this writing, is still broadcasting on 650 AM WSM in Nashville, Tennessee, started blasting country music into homes in Maine and California in 1925—and was likely Woody Guthrie's first introduction to the genre when he was growing up in Oklahoma; New York's 77 AM WABC brought a taste of big city life to people living in shacks in Wyoming. Yes, there was often crackling during the day caused by the waves' wrestling matches with storms and sunspots, but this only added to the organic, ephemeral nature of the listening experience: The sound, delicate and prone to disturbance, was fighting its way across land and sea all so you could hear Casey Kasem's dulcet tones. If you had to play with your radio's knob or the antenna in order to get the least static-y sound, it only made the end listening experience feel all the more earned.

Frequency modulation radio, a.k.a. FM, was in development since before World War II, but it didn't amass a loyal following until the late 1970s; it was in the 60s, however, that it became a way for countercul-ture music lovers to get on the radio when the FCC had already handed out most of the frequencies in the AM band. FM, which operated at much higher frequencies that were less prone to natural interference, had about ten times AM's range. This extra space meant that the sound waves could carry more information. With all that additional room to play with, FM broadcasters put out their signals in stereo, so that people with FM receivers could get a sound much fuller than the tinny one that AM listeners were accustomed to—that thin, old-telephone sound today sometimes used as an effect in modern pop songs.

College radio DJs and the non-mainstream music aficionados broadcasting on the FM airwaves shirked the tight formulas that had become de rigueur on the AM band—the Top 40 countdowns and the same songs in rotation every hour, each one bookended by ten-minute commercials. Instead, they used the stations to play experimental music and embraced offbeat talk programs. The content could afford to be esoteric, if only because the people who owned FM receivers were few and far between. If you were listening to FM in the 60s, you were considered to be kind of weird. But you were probably proud of that fact.

In 1962, according to the FCC, there were only 983 commercially operated FM stations; by 1975, there were close to four thousand. The shift happened when FM operators began embracing some of AM's formatted ways, and people started to catch on that music sounded way better in stereo. There was also the fact that manufacturers began selling affordable radios that could pick up both bands. Once listeners had a choice between hearing something full and rich or something flat and tinny, they sought out music on the FM channels, leaving AM stations to pick up sports and talk shows—programs where sound quality wasn't so important. In 1979, the New York disco station WKTU FM made news for bumping the AM channel WABC from its long-held #1 slot.

By the time that the FCC approved some of the AM stations to also broadcast in stereo in 1982, listeners had already made the switch and had little reason to go back to their old ways. AM's future was further complicated by the fact that you had to have the right equipment in order to hear the richer AM stereo tones. This required going out and buying a new, often expensive receiver that had to correspond with whichever of the handful of transmitter systems your favorite station used. There was no AM transmitter/receiver standardization until 1993 in the US, by which point there was little point to hearing AM in stereo unless the thing that bothered you most about Don Imus was his timbre.

Today, many MP3 devices with radio components don't offer AM stations at all, largely because the AM signal requires a transmitter that's bulkier than FM's, and the signal tends to receive interference from nearby MP3 circuitry.

That doesn't mean that old AM transistors don't have any use in modern times. When Bill Schweber of *Electronic Engineering Times* took one of his old ones for a trip around his home in 2008, he found it was unexpectedly useful—despite the fact that he couldn't actually tune in to any stations.

"What really struck me were the specific sounds I heard," he writes. "There was the whine from the electric motor of a nearby service cart; you could judge its RPM by the pitch. There were loud snaps from switches in nearby heavy machinery. PC power supplies and display oscillators added their own noise to the mix. I could have decided to toss the radio . . . but in today's world, it's all about spin and repositioning your assets and attributes. I took out my Brother electronic labeler, made up an 18-point-size label that clearly announced '500-to 1,600-kHz RF Sniffer,' and felt I had done the radio justice."

ANALOG CLOCKS

Devices based on sundials; used to display time with two mechanical arms, one shorter than the other, pointing to the hour and minute, respectively (some had a third hand which tracked the passing seconds); minutes were calculated by multiplying the number closest to the big hand by five. Sometimes required winding. Sometimes read using terms like "quarter" or "half." Sometimes necessitated doing math by assigning values to letters such as X, V, and I. Conveniently, the hands moved in the direction known as "clockwise."

ANONYMITY

Living an existence that warranted only two status updates; three, if you got married. (*Also see Privacy*)

ANSWERING MACHINES

Devices with an insatiable appetite for the names, numbers, and times of phone calls.

• • •

Today, recluses get a bad rap. Once, however, there was perfectly good reason never to leave the house: What if someone called?

Sure, when you were home, there was only a light drizzle of telemarketers and wrong numbers. You occasionally checked the dial tone, just to make sure it was still there. But who knew what crazy things would happen if you ventured into the outer realm of people taking part in this thing they called life? The fridge's light might go on even with the door closed; your dog could read Karl Marx. And the phone? It would certainly go berserk. The telephone company would probably cut off your service all together, incredulous that one human being could be so popular. No amount of sunlight could be worth that risk.

In the 1970s, thanks to the invention of call forwarding, when answering services became available to the masses, it was no longer necessary to run to the other side of the house in order not to miss a call (after just having sprinted downstairs to add the fabric softener). If you did miss that call, an operator would pick it up and then relay the message when you phoned in later to check on your popularity level. No, it wasn't cheap to hire a company to answer your incoming calls, but important people had to make such sacrifices.

It was, at last, a way to avoid those long, thin evenings in front of the telly (one doesn't need to go outside in order to be worldly, does one?) without panicking over the possibility of missing a call from a certain suitor. Or Ed McMahon. On occasion, this person might be one and the same.

There was, however, a certain awkwardness to having a third person involved in all of your communiqués. "You'd get to know the people at the service after a while," says Nancy, a sixty-year-old lifelong New Yorker. "I remember getting into these blowout fights with my boyfriend. He'd hang up on me and then I'd call back and the answering service would pick up and I'd find myself yelling at the people at the service, 'Let it ring through! Make him pick up!'" Usually, they'd comply with this kind of request. Almost all the operators were women.

Answering machines had been used by businesses for several decades, but they were not widely available to consumers until the 1980s. They gained popularity as people realized that it was a one-time purchase that amounted to a fraction of the cost of a year of their old service's bills. Phone usage surged in the 80s as people caught on to the idea that you could make the requisite calls to exes and in-laws at odd hours without actually having to speak to anyone, provided they remembered to turn on their machines. By 1988, more than a quarter of all US households had answering machines. "I remember asking one of the women at the answering service if she thought I'd be better off with a machine. She said, 'How am I supposed to respond to that question?'" recalls Nancy.

It was undeniable, however, that answering machines offered an array of features that no service could replicate. In addition to picking up your missed calls, the devices could screen callers. They could also be used to say hello to your parakeet while you were at work. And if you realized you left the oven on, you might call to see if the machine picked up—a good indication that your home had yet to go up in flames.

Some machines required that the outgoing message be at least thirty seconds long in order to give the recording device time to kick in. In order to avoid hang-ups, machine owners went to great lengths to entertain their callers, often using the outgoing message to display their limerick-writing abilities or their Italian vocabulary or to broadcast their favorite Santana tracks. Many used those lengthy seconds to spell out every step of the message-capturing-and-retrieval process.

"Hello. Barbara isn't home right now. You have reached her answering machine . . ." they'd intone, assuaging the caller's fear of reaching Barbara's blender.

The early machine used an audio cassette for the outgoing message and another for the incoming ones. What would sitcom writers have done if it weren't for those little tapes and all the inevitably embarrassing messages they recorded? Fortunately, there were plenty of ways that a message could get lost before you'd have to crawl through the window to retrieve a tape: Sometimes the tapes broke; often they cut off during a message. It wasn't long, however, before these devices begat digital progeny that put no limit on how long an incoming message could be. A mixed blessing, to be sure.

In the 2000s, we use voicemail—if we bother to leave a message at all: Talking requires a level of exertion second only to listening. At least voicemail is dependable enough that you don't have to run in order to avoid losing a call. Actually, the fact that you usually have your phone on your person means that it's hard to miss a call to begin with. Still, that doesn't mean you always want to answer the darn thing—or, for that, matter, be bothered to take the time to listen to your accumulated messages. So, please don't leave your name, number, and the time that you called. Just send a text. *Baci, ciao.*

APPENDICITIS SCARS

Scars anywhere from one to six inches in length, located on the right side of the belly and visible when doing the YMCA dance while wearing low-waisted jeans; decrease in ubiquity thanks to laparoscopic surgeries that don't leave the same telltale line, medications that can help avoid surgeries, and improved diagnostics that lead to fewer unnecessary slicings.

ARCADES

Storefronts that predate the migration of video games to basements and computer monitors, filled with consoles designed to help children understand concepts, such as military defense (Atari Missile Command) and feminism (Ms. Pac-Man); effective in helping to cultivate a nascent taste for casinos.

ASBESTOS

Natural mineral that, to the disappointment of many a personal-injury lawyer, was banned by some countries in the late twentieth and early twenty-first centuries; formerly used widely in ceiling insulation, drywall, flooring, and most other permanent edifices occupied by indoor-based humans. Known for its convenience, effectiveness, and low cost; pesky side effects of exposure included lung disease and death.

BALD SPOTS

The result of involuntary loss of head hair, visible when a man who was so afflicted chose neither to wear a toupee nor shave off the rest of his scant cranial offerings. "Sometimes referred to as androgenetic alopecia. This may be identified by the four basic patterns of hair loss: the 'Widow's Peak,' where the hair recedes up the temples, leaving a narrow strip of hair down the center of the head; the 'Naked Crown,' where the hair recedes more quickly in the centre and more slowly at the sides; the 'Domed Forehead,' where the whole of the hairline recedes; and the 'Monk's Patch,' where a bald patch grows at the top and back of the head. If a Widow's Peak and a Monk's Patch occur on the same head, the eventual result is a small 'Fantasy Island' of hair just above the forehead, surrounded by an expanse of bare scalp."—Bald! From Hairless Heroes to Comic Combovers. (Also see Comb-overs)

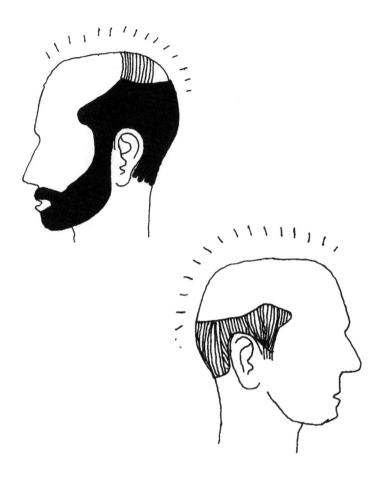

BELLHOPS

Hat-wearing hotel employees paid to carry bags and be discrete. Propriety dictated that: "Unless you have a light bag or the hotel is especially busy, don't deprive him of his tip by taking your bags yourself."—*Emily Post's Etiquette*

BLACKBOARDS

Large black, green, or dark gray wall-mounted boards made of either slate or enamel-coated steel; used primarily in schools, for either edification or torture.

· · ·

It's hard not to have complicated feelings about the big rectangles that loomed large in the front of classrooms for so long. Blackboards certainly had their share of pros—they gave us permission to write on the wall, acted like larger-than-life Etch A Sketches, and insured that teachers would have to spend some part of every class with their backs turned to the students. When your name got called to the board and you found yourself standing framed by that black expanse, you couldn't help but feel kind of important—unless you were being forced to write one sentence over and over again, à la Bart in the opening credits of *The Simpsons*. That was when you suddenly remembered the hand cramps that came on as soon as you gripped a piece of chalk, the sneeze-inducing dust, the inimitable screeches that the board would sometimes inadvertently produce while being written upon, and the fact that facing it meant that a room full of people was staring at your behind.

For more than a century, the blackboard was really the only way to easily disseminate written information to a group of people all at once. In the early nineteenth century, American schools began experimenting with using slate slabs in classrooms—the United States Military Academy at West Point in New York is thought to be one of the first schools to have used them. It was a blessing for teachers who no longer had to copy out problems by hand for each student. Few other tools have been used so effectively by everyone from kindergarteners to physicists to football players. In the mid-twentieth century, green became the new black, as steel boards coated with moss-colored porcelain enamel began to replace the traditional slate boards. No matter the color, they had the odd quality of being kind of pleasant to wash; there was a Zen aspect to wiping a soft chamois or a wet sponge over the dusty remnants of math problems, and the cleaning of the erasers usually meant banging them to make irresistible indoor clouds. And we wonder why so many of us ended up with asthma . . .

But today, we're no longer so dependent on the dusty behemoths we all knew and scrubbed. In a world filled with Dry Erase markers, PowerPoint presentations, high-speed printers, and interactive whiteboards (computer-projector hybrids), teachers have many options for conveying ideas to a classroom, making the blackboard far less of a necessity.

So you can finally sit down, Bart.

BLIND DATES

Romantic rendezvous at which you don't know anything about the person you're supposed to be courting.

• • •

Smoke and mirrors have long had a place in romance. For ages, we've made ourselves up and shaved ourselves down; we've surgically enhanced the things we can and covered up the things we can't. We've courted each other by the forgiving light of candles, and the nothings we whisper wouldn't be so sweet if not for Binaca.

Indeed, we've become experts in various scripts of untruths: Yes, it was good for me; Really, I've never felt this way before; No, you don't look fat.

The blind date was a proceeding that required much of this kind of playacting. On these assignations, neither party knew much about the other before meeting up at a bar or café, resulting in so many minutes of awkwardly scoping out other patrons and pretending to be nonchalant, but really searching for a glimmer of recognition. The rendezvous that followed was a sales fest, with each participant trying to present the best aspects of her or his product while downplaying the rest . . . kind of like a pharmaceutical commercial—one with children running in fields with puppies and kites, omitting the voiceover listing the medication's dysenteric side effects.

Today, however, relationships have a larger degree of transparency than ever, with technological advances allowing more potential for honesty than was an option in unions of yesteryear. Thanks to computers, we now need to contemplate entirely new ways that we want to be intimate with the people we love . . . or not. Are you comfortable giving your lover your password? Your PIN? Access to your computer at all? Rare is the suspicious spouse who hasn't tried to log in to his wife's e-mail account, or the girlfriend who doesn't surreptitiously check her honey's browser history.

Most notably, the opportunity for navigating deceptions and disclosures using the Web is completely changing the way potential lovers learn about one another before they meet face to face. The idea of a chance encounter or recognizing a date only by the carnation in his lapel have become . . . quaint. If a friend sets you up with someone and you don't automatically look for his image on Google, check his "relationship" status on Facebook, and make sure his name isn't listed on CheaterNews.com or TheDickList.com (the modern answers to stocks and pillories), one might question if you're fit to date at all. Instead of painting a picture of your ideal self, much of a first date is now spent trying to assess how much the person across the table actually knows about you. In the age of Internet dating, wannabe paramours who spend weeks weaving intricate false representations of themselves in their online dating profiles—using photos taken from *juuust* the right angle—can quickly be brought down by a site like TrueDater.com, where previously deceived online conquests report how Mr. Right on Match.com is, in the flesh, actually Mr. Fat, Married, and Republican.

Love may still be blind, but dating? Not so much.

BODY HAIR

Corporeal fuzz found primarily in the armpit, leg, facial, chest, back, and genital areas.

. . .

Getting ready for a date once involved little more than a blow-dryer, a razor, and a handful of products that could be found at the drugstore (or the grocery store, if you were one of those mayonnaise-conditioner people). No need to worry about the fact that you were sprouting little rain forests over each eye.

Today, however, a primper's routine might involve spending several hours and more than a few dollars on professional services: eyebrow threading, lip bleaching, armpit waxing, pubic hair removal via lasers—even those little fluffy fellas near the hairline are likely to get pulled. Hairstyles come and go, but there's a big difference between altering a do's look—Ringlets! Bikini! Van Dyke!—and deciding to get rid of the stuff all together.

Being hairy has become like choosing to be fat or not wanting to part with your bulky CRT computer screen—we're obsessed with whittling everything down to the bare minimum so that we can get as close to not existing as possible, if only because it makes our big cars feel roomier, and our post–*Pumping Iron* pecs all the more visible. Hair just really isn't so necessary, so what good is it? Fuzzy bodies now hint at a kind of shame not felt by those who've epilated in order to show off every curve and crease. Only he with something to hide would wear a sweater at the beach.

The popularity of extreme grooming regimes has led to the wider acceptance of depilation in areas that once would've seemed vain. No longer does the man with a unibrow need either to pluck in secret or resign himself to the fact that he'll have to compensate for unsightly sub-forehead hair with extra personality and vim. Why go through all that effort when there's a perfectly good waxing place on the corner?

The hairlessness vogue is most apparent below the belt, perhaps resulting from attempts to emulate the look of porn stars, without resorting to surgery or a wardrobe of buttless chaps. And yet, the only people among us who are naturally sans pubic hair are also the people who can wear party hats sans irony. Yes, we all want to seem young . . . but that young? Whatever the reason, pubic hair removal is a custom that, like foot binding, very likely will lead children to permanently affect their bodies. They may never know the mixture of excitement and fear experienced when those kinky hairs first sprout. Laser hair removal can help banish those hairs for good; waxing can also curb the regrowth process. In other words, if you're a twenty-first-century child, you might never catch sight of a little bit of fuzz at the bottom of a bathing suit, or believe that there was a time when it seemed like there could be no relationship in a beauty parlor more feudal and embarrassing than the one between pedicurist and patron. You'll never have tactile proof that your redheaded roommate used your bar of soap.

At Wanda's European Skin Care Center in Manhattan, there is a special menu for children's services, which has a website that advertises "'Virgin' waxing for children eight years old and up who have never shaved before. Virgin hair can be waxed so successfully that growth can be permanently stopped in just two to six sessions! Save your child a lifetime of waxing . . . and put the money in the bank for her college education instead!"

BOOKS

Bound collections of papers, which, said E. M. Forster, "have to be read. It is the only way of discovering what they contain. A few savage tribes eat them, but reading is the only method of assimilation revealed to the West."

• • •

They smelled of dying trees emitting their last breaths. Hardcovered ones often came wearing jackets that were easily marred or lost; the paperback variety had spines that showed the cracks of overuse and pages that turned sallow and brittle with age. They never were the least bit

appreciative of all the shelf space they were given, and really were awfully expensive, compared to your average doorstop or coaster. Municipalities devoted entire buildings to soporific tomes and searched people's bags for them upon exiting (despite the fact that they were encouraging people to take them without paying). Students were particularly susceptible to their wily charms, and so often ended up spending their pittances supporting their habit, even going so far as to invest in thick glasses and particleboard bookcases. It all seemed a big scheme that produced one long, sweet dollar for every publisher that hung up a shingle, and any sorry hack who knew how to double-space a document and address manila envelopes.

Long before used bookstores became headquarters for the world's movers and shakers, there was concern about the possible effects of the written word. In a 1994 lecture, the writer and philosopher Umberto Eco reminded his addressees of Frollo from *The Hunchback of Notre Dame*: "Comparing a book with his old cathedral, he says: '*Ceci tuera cela*' (The book will kill the cathedral, the alphabet will kill images)." Mr. Eco went on to compare this to Socrates's tale of the Pharaoh Thamus, who discouraged the invention of writing, warning that if people knew how to put pen to paper, they'd no longer memorize anything, and this would lead to torpid minds and a weakened civilization.

Indeed.

Ever since electronic and audiobooks began gaining attention in the late 1900s, there has been speculation that a new *ceci* might finally do the *tuera*-ing. Hopes were further stoked in 2000 when Stephen King's digitally released thriller *Riding the Bullet* sold six hundred thousand copies in just forty-eight hours. At the end of 2005, the audiobook industry's annual revenue was approaching $1 billion a year. Just months later, Sony introduced the Sony Reader Digital Book, which was a kind of portable computer that could download books; in 2007, Amazon followed suit with a similar device called the Kindle (a name which brought to mind the pleasant image of burning paper). Books that might've been filled with ideas were finally being distilled down to little more than strings of zeroes and ones; in an increasingly crowded world, why store concepts and couplets in objects that take up so much mass? A story that exists only on an LCD screen still offers up a plot that can be mined by a screenwriter.

Yet the popularity of these reusable gadgets, which were roughly the same size as a book, suggested that there maybe were some people out there who weren't yet ready to forgo the experience of holding text in their hands; perhaps they were just embracing a way to do it without killing trees and getting paper cuts. Some prayed that these devices had solved the problem—even Mr. Eco, who's made millions from the sales of old-fashioned paperbacks, said "I receive too many books every week. If the computer network succeeds in reducing the quantity of published books, this would be a paramount cultural improvement."

Many, however, grumbled that there was no way that these miniscreens could ever supplant the elegant simplicity of a book. The invention of sliding doors, they argued, didn't render hinges unnecessary; people still devoted their lives to painting even after the development of photography. There were also those who straddled both sides, arguing that one format might be able to inform the other, and vice versa: Isn't it possible that out-of-print books could find new life in a digitized form? Perhaps texts that were initially released online would end up getting printed for posterity?

Maybe. The only problem with these postulations is that they all start with the basic assumption that people want to read, and that kind of thinking might just make an "ass" out of "u" and "mption." According to a 2007 poll conducted by the Associated Press, more than a quarter of Americans read less than one book per year; if they're reading at all, it usually involves skimming text on computer screens laden with bullet points, short paragraphs, and pictures. This looks like adieu, *cela*.

BOOM BOXES

Also known as "ghetto blasters"; cassette-cum-radio players that

BOOM BOX

GHETTO BLASTER

were often balanced on the shoulder, "blasting" one's music tastes to everyone in the "ghetto."

• • •

Matt Steck, a student at Penn State, likes to share his music. In particular, he likes to share it with people who are out shopping at the Berkshire Mall in Reading, Pennsylvania. On any given afternoon, you are likely to see him there blasting new wave tunes from his 1983 JVC boom box. The man's never met a D-battery he didn't like.

"I don't do it to be different. I just like the sound quality. People are always amazed at how good it sounds," says Mr. Steck, age twenty. "It's also a way to be social. I mean, I might not be playing music that everyone around me wants to hear, but at least I'm interacting with people. And maybe I'll end up playing something you didn't know you'd like."

Back in the house where he grew up, Mr. Steck has more than twenty vintage boom boxes that he's collected from garage sales. There are ones that have a single cassette player, and ones that have two or even three. Some models have detachable speakers, while others can play records, inserted vertically. Most of them cost more than an MP3 player would today.

Boom boxes, first introduced in the late 1970s, were quickly adopted by disco-goers and break-dancers as totems of power; they were mammoth machines that refused to be ignored, whether that meant using them to get a girl's attention (à la Lloyd Dobler playing "In Your Eyes" outside his crush's window in *Say Anything*) or asserting power in a pizza joint (a potentially fatal move by Radio Raheem in *Do the Right Thing*).

If few people have ever complained to Mr. Steck about his attempt to serenade the world with his Blondie and Huey Lewis mixtapes, it might be because most people around him don't hear any of it. Today's public places are flooded with people living in their own little aural universes. Personal music players give us autonomy, but they also tune out the rest of the world. It's nearly impossible to have a conversation with strangers when you're wearing headphones, let alone do the Running

Man to the same rhythm as someone else.

Boom boxes forced social interaction. Yes, they may have sometimes been disruptive, but at least they were egalitarian: Anyone could whip one out if they wanted to determine which song everyone else would hear. The result was that every block had its own shifting soundtrack and flavor, and conversation and dancing with other people were possible in a way that just doesn't occur when everyone in the park is listening to their own pocket-sized device.

Of course, wielding a boom box took more self-confidence (not to mention strength) than using an iPod. Those who couldn't hack it in public might've settled for playing Ghettoblaster on the Commodore 64—a game where a character gained points by collecting batteries and tapes to put in his ersatz boom box. Others invested in handheld radios or Walkmen if they needed to satiate their yen for music on the go. But the boom box toters knew that walking down the street with a large and loud device balanced on your shoulder was in and of itself a reward, no matter what tunes you were blasting. "I had to build up the guts to do it, but once I did, I found it was really exhilarating," says Mr. Steck. "It's a real rush. And it seems much more human than walking around with little buds in your ears. That's the total opposite of social. To me, that's not what music is about."

BUFFERING

Endlessly aggravating pauses that occurred onscreen while watching choppy playback of online clips and films, usually accompanied by an image of an hourglass, a rotating circle, or a colored horizontal bar; often resulted in basketball games that looked like groups of robots playing freeze tag; most common before high-speed Internet connections were available outside the workplace. Inspired bilious YouTube users to post proclamations like VideoSuperMaster's "One day Satan found out about buffering and said to himself, 'Even I think that is too evil.'"

CAMCORDERS

Handheld devices that recorded family events onto video tapes (see page 176); turned every parent into Steven Spielberg—at least, in their own eyes.

• • •

The 1980s brought us the Betacam and VHS-C tapes—mini recordable VHS cassette tapes. These two technologies meant that events could be recorded with just a portable apparatus that could turn anyone into a cameraman—be it a naked lover, a puppet-wielding tot, or a misanthropic cousin eager to have something to hide behind at a wedding. Editing, however, wasn't possible for the average home-movie maker, which is part of the reason that the devices were more popular for capturing family events than they were for attempting to make actual plotted amateur movies. The technology replaced the cans of film and carousel projectors that were once lugged out in order to relive a ski trip or reunion or a wedding; it didn't necessarily make the rewatching any more interesting, but it did make the turnaround time a lot faster. You could head home and relive every moment of the office party all over again that very night! That is when you decided to off yourself.

Groups of parents at the weekend soccer game began looking like crowds of news crews, thanks to the bulky recorders balanced on their shoulders. They resembled so many myopic pirates, one eye squinting while the other stayed glued to the viewfinder. This method of recording created a dilemma for many a parent: Was it worth experiencing your daughter as Ado Annie through a tiny square while squinting, or did you enjoy the moment to its fullest and not worry about capturing it for posterity? Did you trust your own filming ability over the skills of the gangly sophomore who once forgot to remove the lens cap?

Footage captured by a camcorder that required a small cassette could only be viewed if transferred to a bigger tape. By that point, however, you'd lost the oblong sticker that was supposed to label the thing and instead had to resort to masking tape or duct tape, which had a tendency to eventually peel off, leaving crusty bits. Once they fell off, you had to watch each tape again so that you knew how to label it. This activity inevitably led to the appearance of old footage of a grandparent that was sure to cause some sniffles. Often, however, there was also the appearance of an X-rated cassette that would end up in the trash, if only because "Positions to be avoided because they make me look really fat during sex" didn't fit on a label.

CAPITALIZATION

Letters written in the upper case (a term derived from the location they occupied in printers' cabinets); used when referring to the first person singular in the subject form, at the start of a proper noun, in acronyms, and at the beginning of a sentence; when typing, required the considerable exertion of holding down two keys at once. (NB: Not an indication of yelling.) According to a 2005 study conducted by Norwegian researcher Richard Ling, less than 20 percent of text messages contain any sort of upper case letters. (*Also see Full Words*)

CAR CIGARETTE LIGHTERS

A heating element located on the dashboard, introduced into cars in the 1920s and used exclusively to light cigars and cigarettes; sworn enemy of the air freshener.

CASH

Legal tender made from fiber-based paper. Also known as dough, moolah, dinero, dosh, paper, greenbacks, clams, beans, bucks, dead presidents, spondulicks, lettuce, cheese, bread, the long green, scrilla, smackers, or bacon.

• • •

Take a good whiff of that greenback—if you actually have any in your wallet, that is. The aroma might just take you back to a time of savings pass books (in lieu of an online savings account), rolling quarters (instead of hitting the Coinstar change counting machines), and trips to Europe when you could actually afford a Madeleine.

Everything we know about the dollar is shifting faster than the exchange rate. Bills and coins used to be symbols of great wealth, but, today, if you have money to spare, it's likely that you'll hardly have any bills on you, if only because sitting on that fat a wallet will lead to sciatica. Want to buy your house in cold hard cash? If the seller accepts it, you'll need some serious biceps in order to heave that many bills over the threshold. Even the color that launched a dozen nicknames—the green stuff, lettuce, cabbage—is itself dated. The new twenties are kind of pinkish and periwinkle, and the new fives are . . . um, is anyone still able to live off of bills other than twenties?

Coins aren't faring any better. Pennies, once so inexpensive to make that their production actually turned a profit for the government, now cost more than a cent to make; because the pre–1982 ones were mostly copper, they are now worth nearly three times as much as the one-cent printed on them. Some military bases have already experimented with getting rid of the smallest coins. Things aren't looking much better for nickels: In 2008, they cost almost ten cents each to produce.

In the mid-2000s, Las Vegas and Atlantic City both introduced slot machines that dispense vouchers instead of clanking coins, which somehow seems to rob the soul as much as it does the wallet. Fake money seems doomed as well: Some editions of Monopoly have completely done away with the colored money. As if the banker's job wasn't sweet enough, she now gets to go all Arthur Andersen on her opponents, inserting players' "credit cards" in a handheld machine, checking a balance which only she can see, and then deducting or adding denominations (which, in the new version, are seriously adjusted for inflation). It's all a little too much like real life.

Checks are facing a similar demise, replaced instead by online transactions that are instant and therefore give the money's recipients more confidence that the funds actually exist. Utilities still take them, but in many stores they're now about as useful as trying to buy toilet paper with a handshake. Still, we do love our credit cards. Sure you can't fold them into ad hoc bowties, but they are quite handy. They buy us books on Amazon! Movie tickets! College educations! They, too, however, may soon be good for little more than tooth picking. We're already seeing the black strips on their backs replaced with small chips that can be waved in front of a cash register, rendering the entire swiping action unnecessary. Those thumbnail-sized chips can be embedded in many things other than pieces of flat plastic: Thanks to technology currently being tested in several states, a simple tap of a cell phone will likely be the way your average shopper will pay for things in coming years. After that, the next logical development would seem to be technology that automatically deducts funds from your checking account when you simply *think* about what you want to buy. Wait—isn't that what the Internet is for?

CDs

Discs capable of storing more than an hour of digital music—which, once, seemed like an eternity.

• • •

So long, CDs—we hardly knew how to open ye.

But we tried. Really, we did. We used our teeth, our nails, our steak knives. We sometimes broke off your jewel cases' covers in frustration, and then slipped you into a Case Logic sleeve. We eventually invested in a contraption made specifically to slice open the force fields which kept you shielded from a world that would scratch you, mark you with Sharpies, copy you, and ultimately place you facedown on the windowsill to keep the pigeons away (hey, it worked).

When compact discs were first introduced in 1982, they resembled shiny artifacts from the future—the kind of thing a robot would eat for breakfast. They were impressive little objects: hefty double albums like the Clash's *London Calling* could be distilled down to one twelve-centimeter, eighty-minute disc that gave the listener the ability to skip the least-preferred tracks. Yet the coasterlike devices also somehow made music seem . . . smaller. Once they were shrunk down to fit inside a five-inch plastic square, album covers were no longer so effective. But with all those Columbia House offers to buy ten discs for one penny—and no commitment to buy more!—did it really matter what the cover art looked like?

Even if many music buffs never quite took the form seriously (record stores never billed themselves as "CD shops," no matter how many jewel cases they stocked), it was hard not to like the way the uniform cases had bindings that stacked so nicely, displaying titles that were far easier to read than the ones on LP spines. But extract one CD from the bottom of that little ziggurat of discs in the corner and it suddenly seemed that it was on a mission to divorce itself from its case. This problem was especially prevalent in cars—somehow, the trip between the front seat and the six-CD changer in the trunk always resulted in some errant Madonna album taking up residence in the *Reality Bites* soundtrack case. Under the seat, the tabs on the plastic floret that stuck in the hole of the Pearl Jam disc had cracked off and were rattling around in the cup holder. Then there was the Prince CD that had been so lovingly placed in a sleeve in the visor, but nevertheless was now playing like was it was 1999—nine, nine, nine. There were a couple of remedies you might employ to fix the scratches, but you should probably test them out on that Ace of Base disc first.

In the end, MP3s are a more forgiving format, even if they're harder to wrap up and put under the Hanukkah bush. They don't scratch or collect dust or require that you pull over if you want to hear a new artist. They don't have great cover art, but CDs already brought down any expectations we had that great music should be paired with interesting images.

There's still a market for blank CDs—they are one method of transporting digital media from one computer to another, for example. But music CDs are not long for this world. In 2007, when their sales plunged by more than 20 percent, many music stores stopped selling CD singles, and America's Consumer Electronics Association reported that devices for linking MP3 players to car stereos were swiftly outselling CD players.

But those who are getting ready to whimper about yet another nail in the record store coffin can go ahead and put those hankies away. Steady increases in music downloads might indeed mean that there are fewer brick-and-mortar places for music geeks to congregate and browse, but many of these old stores are finding ballast in a music format that predates even the CD: LPs. While CD sales are diminishing every year, music lovers who are nostalgic for a form of music that they can hold and cherish are going back to vinyl. In 2008, 1.8 million vinyl records left store shelves—more than in any other year since Nielsen began tracking their sales in 1991. That might amount to little more than the number of LPs that Michael Jackson's *Thriller* sold in one week the year it came out, but still . . .

CESAREANS FOR EMERGENCIES ONLY

Procedure for delivering babies done only when all other options were exhausted, and not performed in order to accommodate business trips, tee-off times, or desire for a tummy tuck. Between 1989 and 1999, the US cesarean rate quintupled, although the rate of deliveries that were considered "risky" stayed steady.

CHECKS

Oblong paper bank notes that were interminably "in the mail" and often a topic of conversation on Fridays. Check delivery by postal service allowed for a certain grace period in which one could amass the necessary funds. Sometimes bounced ones were displayed on the wall behind a deli cashier. Often decorated with monograms, pinstripes, or scenes from *Winnie the Pooh*.

COMB-OVERS

Arcs of flapping hairs balanced on the shiny domes of balding men. Long a symbol of geekdom; a hairdo that meant you were old, unhip, or both.

• • •

People wondered about the life choices made by the man who favored this hairstyle: Did he actually grow one side of his hair long in order to facilitate that look? Did his scalp get sticky when he lacquered the hairs with Aqua Net?

The main question, however, was simply, "Does he really think he's fooling anyone?"

Sadly, comb-overs often developed without the wearer realizing it. It was a hairdo that could evolve over time—there you were combing and parting your hair every day, combing and parting, combing and parting, and then one morning you realize that your widow's peak is running away from your eyebrows, and the hairs that are slipping through the comb's teeth are coming from the *side* of your head, not the *top*. Yes, you could just cut it and go with the horseshoe look, but is it rude to expose your shiny pate to the world? Maybe you could just soften the look a little by covering it with just a couple hairs . . .

Some people actually cultivated their comb-overs, viewing them as hairstyles as good as any other. In 1975, Eric Oakley penned the cleverly titled book *A Method of Disguising Your Male Baldness Using Your Own Hair from the Sides* which offered a detailed analysis of the best ways to construct a comb-over. "We now have a great alternative that can be adapted as we get older," he wrote, going onto describe the comb-over as "the only practical and masculine way to disguise male baldness." The book answers many a comb-over-wearer's most pressing questions. What happens if the hair at the sides recedes even further? "Simply lower your parting." What if it rains? "You will need to use a hat."

In 1977, an Orlando, Florida, father and son went one step further and actually patented a comb-over process that involved covering the bald spot with flaps of hair from both the sides and the back of the head. It was neat, required no synthetic products, and lacked the admission of vanity that hair plugs or a toupee implied. For many years, it was former New York Mayor Rudy Giuliani's preferred hairdo. Homer Simpson all but trademarked the look. Donald Trump has constructed his with such skill that experts worldwide have tried (and failed) to figure out on which side the hair originates.

Of course, ridding oneself of head hair completely was always an option, but going totally hair-free was a major statement—a look that could best be pulled off if you had a singular presence and lofty goals: to fight crime while sucking lollipops; to leave the kitchen floors glistening; to adopt Little Orphan Annie. It wasn't a look for John over in accounting.

But when swarms of baby boomers started experiencing hair loss in the 1980s, head shaving started to seem like a viable solution. The comb-over began to look extra fusty—as did any kind of bald spot that didn't take over the entire head.

"I'm a former comb-over wearer," says Howard Brauner, founder of Bald Guyz, a company that makes scalp-care products for bald men. "I did the comb-over for twelve years. I thought it looked like I had hair. I'd use two different hair sprays. It'd take half an hour. But then one day in the heat, the products melted and my hair fell flat and I realized how ridiculous it was. I went to the barber and said 'take it all off.' Being bald is clean. It's sexy."

Even non-balding men have appropriated the look, often referring to themselves as BBC, or "Bald by Choice." These premature head-shavers aren't just swimming with the tide—they are going faster than it; with the comb-over bobbing sadly in their wake, it will only become increasingly difficult to differentiate between geeks and Siamese kings.

COMMERCIALS

Short advertisement films that could not be skipped but allowed a moment to get a snack during *Divorce Court*. Generated enough revenue for stations to air shows on network TV for free without making Paula, Simon, and Randy drink three liters of Coke on camera every hour.

CORRECTION FLUID

Second only to prayer when it came to ensuring error-free correspondence.

• • •

Once upon a time, you kept a little odiferous bottle in your desk that could make so many problems fade away.

You also probably had a container of correction fluid.

In the days before the invention of the word processor, a row of Xs or a bottle of Wite-Out were the two easiest ways to correct a typo. The history of correction fluid contains the story of one of the twentieth century's most successful female entrepreneurs. Bette Nesmith Graham, a typist at a bank in Texas, started using white tempera paint in the 1950s to cover up typing errors after she saw how the Christmas window painters at the bank where she worked simply painted over their mistakes. Other secretaries caught on to Ms. Graham's little secret and asked her to make bottles for them, too. After consulting with a chemistry teacher and a paint manufacturer, she perfected the formula, bottled it at home with the help of her son, and began selling it. She first called her creation Mistake Out, but then changed it to Liquid Paper. By the late 1960s, her company had expanded to a factory and was seeing sales of more than a million bottles a year. When she sold the company in 1979, Ms. Graham pocketed more than $47 million (much of which eventually went to her son, Michael Nesmith, a.k.a. the wool-hat wearing member of the Monkees). There were big things in store for the company. Heyhey, correction pens!

Early versions of Liquid Paper and its main competitor, Wite-Out (1971), were far from perfect. They required multiple coats in order to be truly opaque; they needed considerable time to dry, and it was easy to see the original mistake under the white covering if you held the document up to the light. The various brands of correction fluid would also smudge when they came in contact with the requisite spelling-error induced tears. Non-water-soluble versions hit the market in the 80s, but the containers had a tendency to dry out quickly, resulting in crusty bits around the top of the bottle that would inevitably end up stuck onto your page. Other times, the application brush would clump up with the product, sometimes getting so dry inside the bottle that the stem refused to come out at all. (Those were times when that other bottle came in handy.)

Brush-on correction fluid wasn't the only player in the typo-mending market. There was Ko-Rec-Type correction film, which, when placed atop the sheet of paper in your typewriter and struck with a letter key, put a precisely shaped white patch over the error—but it wasn't much help if a mistake was more than a word or two. Some brands of paper were purposefully formulated so that they wouldn't completely absorb the ribbon's ink, meaning that you could do a decent job of rubbing out mistakes with an eraser. There was also correction tape on rollers which could dispense a thin layer of dry white film on top of any errors. The era of the word processor then brought us typewriter hybrids that allowed you to read chunks of text on a screen before committing them to paper, and even sometimes came equipped with erasable ink.

But these options couldn't be used as nail polish or as a semi-permanent way to declare who hearted whom on a bathroom door. Nothing could quite compare to a form of error-management that was so elegant in its simplicity and quaint in its ability to only fix mess-ups of minimal size and scope. For most of its lifetime, correction fluid came in only one color, meaning that mistakes made on anything but white paper were all but unfixable. Typos that were larger than a letter or a word or two would result in a slew of sentences that no longer lined up. Despite all kinds of clever maneuvering, this usually meant that all the pages in the document had to be retyped. We were, perhaps, less used to perfection: sometimes it was easier just to live with a slightly awkward sentence than to retype page upon page or slather on coats of correction fluid. Indeed, it was a mistake-repair system that had more of a resemblance to our problem-solving patterns in the non-two-dimensional world than the backspace button. Sometimes it's worth putting in Herculean effort to fix something; sometimes it isn't. Going back and revisiting a mistake, in any case, is rarely easy.

Now, however, it's tempting to blind ourselves to the laws of cause and effect by walking around trying to find the undo button to press when we get into a fender bender or wake up hungover. In the days of correction fluid, we weren't yet plagued with the notion that a quick finger tap could fix everything. You couldn't just backspace your problems. Maybe you could fix things. Maybe you couldn't. Or maybe you'd end up using your fingernail to scrape white stuff off the photocopier glass.

So be it.

CURSIVE WRITING

A form of writing that involved making letters touch each other. Largely impossible for small children to read; adults fared better, but only slightly.

• • •

You were told that learning the hieroglyphs that lined the upper part of your 2nd- or 3rd-grade classroom's walls would make writing faster . . . So why did each letter take so much time to master? It seemed to be purposely nonsensical. The uppercase S looked like a duck (sans bill) swimming to the right. The capital G was some kind of unwieldy creamer, and it was unclear why a big Q was represented by an odd looking number two. Then there was the lowercase K, which masqueraded as a big R; the little N, who started off with an extra M-like arc;

and the capital A, which, inexplicably, was just a big version of a little A. And let us not forget illegitimate F, S, and Z in their lowercase forms: They bore absolutely no resemblance to their printed siblings.

Nevertheless, you humored your teachers long enough each day to develop aching hands, a serious callous near the top joint of your middle finger, and a palm smudged with pencil on its side (badly so if you were a lefty). You tilted the thrice-lined paper as directed, but your head tilted with it, giving you an early introduction to the adult world of neck pain. Hey, if this script stuff is so important, why don't they write books in it? Hmm?

Still, it was easy to see that well-executed cursive—or joined-up letters, as they were called in some other countries—was more aesthetically pleasing than printed lettering, with all its jarring perpendiculars. There was a flow to the lines and flourishes on the capitals, but when executed by small hands, the curlicues and connections between letters so often looked thick and harsh. Adults seemed to each have their own personal style when they wrote out checks or lunchbox notes, but your teacher probably wasn't handing out stickers for individual flair. A homework assignment written in print would often get a lower grade than one executed in the style of the lyrical letters in the workbooks that stacked up. It was an early lesson in the fact that, often, appearances do matter.

It was also one of the first times that it was clear that a person's personality permeated every part of his being, and wasn't merely a factor of what shirt he wore or how many good curse words he knew. One teacher's manual from the 1970s promised that "Handwriting allows the student to see his own spirit in action." That might be overstating it, but there was something about the way one shaped one's letters that seemed to point at a larger aspect of their person being filtered through their fingertips. How was it that your best friend's writing, acquired at the same time and with the same tools as you, seemed so uniquely his own? The kids who seemed to emulate Animal playing the drums at all times so often had cursive practice sheets that looked like some kind of angry cuneiform, no matter how hard they appeared to be trying; the popular girls were able to make very round letters accented with little loops and bubbles and elegant flicks—and never got pink eraser stains on their pages. Those who struggled with the letters would practice their looped Ls and Os while wondering if it was really possible that their penmanship would affect their later lives. It was supposedly the reason Diana Spencer was accepted to her secondary school—and don't *you* want to be a princess one day, Sonny?

"The fact is that girls are ready to learn cursive earlier than boys due to their fine motor skills at an early age," says Milton Moore, a past president of the American Handwriting Analysis Foundation. "Their 'pretty' writing may discourage boys at this early age. It may also be one of the reasons that more boys and men print." However, Mr. Moore says he's seen a noticeable decline in penmanship in the last few decades across both genders. The child who used to carefully practice rows of looping Ls is now seeing how much scribble he can get away with when writing his name; the girl who would once imagine how she'd sign her married moniker today is typing URLs into Google to see if she would be able to register a URL using her first name with her paramour's last. Indeed, it's not uncommon for couples to spend years together without ever learning to recognize each other's handwriting, script or otherwise. Teachers who once judged essays as much on their readability as on their content today welcome papers that are typed, leaving all the more reason to not make an effort to connect letters or add flourishes; in 2006, only 15 percent of SAT takers used connected letters in the exam's essay section.

Cursive's plight, however, comes as no surprise: It's been foreseen—and bemoaned—since long before computers showed up in classrooms. In the late nineteenth century, many complained that metal-nibbed quills, which replaced the feather quills that had been used for some ten centuries, would make it impossible to write neatly. The sobs only got louder at the end of the century, when it seemed that the typewriter would surely doom the existence of the 2-shaped Q and its odd little friends. Soon, there was worry that fountain pens would also be detrimental to cursive writing, since the pauses needed to dip a nib in an inkwell were thought to be necessary if a child was going to develop a steady, neat style of handwriting.

However benign they might seem, ballpoint pens actually ended up being one of the major factors that contributed to today's poor penmanship, with educators often deeming them pestilential. An attractive script, instructors taught, could only be accomplished using a delicate touch—the pen should be held so lightly, students were told, that the teacher should be able to easily knock it out of their hands if she wanted to. With a ballpoint pen, however, you had to bear down on the page in order to make a mark. In her book *Handwriting of the Twentieth Century*, handwriting expert Rosemary Sassoon notes that the styles of cursive that are still taught to children in the 2nd and 3rd and 4th grades "do not work well with free-flowing modern pens. Firmly supported hand positions mean that the hand does not move so freely along the line. Pen lifts must be allowed during longer words, otherwise this combination of the pen and the way we write will strain the muscles of the hand and eventually distort the letters." She goes on to argue that small children who used to learn to hold pencils early on are less likely to develop those same muscles and habits due to the fact that they now so often use ballpoint pens or draw with felt-tipped markers that have to be held at a much more upright angle than more formal writing tools.

Computers are currently taking most of the blame for our diminishing ability to write in longhand in anything other than a kind of print-cursive mélange that's often so rushed we can't read it ourselves. But our society's ever-increasing interest in speed was affecting the legibility of our handwriting long before the first PCs hit our desks. Today's doctors, many of whom weren't schooled in the days when computers were found in every backpack, are so notorious for their poor penmanship that a 2006 report by the National Academies of Science's Institute of Medicine estimated that some seven thousand deaths each year are caused by medical professionals' lousily penned prescriptions.

Many of these chicken-scratchers were learning to write in the 60s, when only about two-thirds of American schools had any kind of formal handwriting program. Still, around that time, Zaner-Bloser, the company that publishes some of the most popular cursive workbooks, was advising that kids spend a healthy forty-five minutes a day on their penmanship; today they recommend just fifteen minutes, although surveys suggest that most grammar schools devote far less time than that. Then again, is there really a point to devoting much more than that to a skill that's almost never required in daily life beyond 4th grade? We might not be able to render the kind of beautiful handwritten pen-and-ink love letters that our grandparents exchanged, but if they'd had Gmail, they would've likely made do with twelve-point Arial as well.

CYCLAMATE

Odorless sugar substitute that was deemed carcinogenic and banned in the US in 1969; the artificial sweetener's mourners argued that even fans of plain old sugar had a 100 percent mortality rate.

DARNING SOCKS

Mending holes in footwear by stretching the torn area over the mouth of a glass or over a maraca-like wood "darning egg" and then weaving threads across the hole to form a kind of netting. According to the 1943 classic *Mending Made Easy*, "If you are a big girl with a new husband's socks to take care of, your alertness to his material needs is sure to make a real hit with him." Fixing high-quality socks was a common evening activity for American mothers and grandmothers who did it with love; today, making cheap new socks from scratch is a common evening activity for Chinese mothers and grandmothers who do it for $1 an hour.

DDT

Chemical used initially during World War II to kill disease-carrying lice and mosquitoes, and, in following decades, sprayed all over the planet to prove our superiority over our insect co-inhabitants; had the pesky side effect of causing cancer, but its main hobby was killing off entire populations of species and thus disturbing the delicate balance of the ecosystem. Usage largely curbed, thanks to the 1995 Stockholm Convention—an event which also unfortunately coincided with an uptick of malaria cases.

DIAL-UP MODEMS

Wired devices that encoded and decoded signals through the telephone cables in order to provide Internet access for the cost of a phone call. (NB: There were no actual dials on the devices.)

• • •

At the end of *2001: Space Odyssey,* the rogue machine HAL sings "A Bicycle Built for Two," but come the 1990s, we all knew the real song of a metamorphosing computer.

It started with a lulling dial tone, then came the little beeps of a phone being dialed, then a series of longer beeps bouncing back and forth, and then static . . . and more static . . . and then screeching that sounded a little bit like your computer might be coughing up phlegm. Is this what it sounds like in space? Will it work this time? Is someone trying to call? Is it going to need to try another number? The agony! The ecstasy! And then . . . "You've got mail!" You'd entered the future.

In 2008, the Pew Research Center reported that the population of dial-up users has been steadily dwindling since 2001, despite the fact that it is still the cheapest way to access the Internet. The number of people using broadband devices surpassed the dial-uppers in 2005; today, only a scant one out of ten Internet users still has to listen to the crackle of devices going through their cyber-handshake ritual. Thanks to volume control options, there are even fewer of us who need to worry about muffling the modem with a pillow in order not to alert the whole household that we're forgoing sleep in order to hang in a chat room with a random grandma in the Midwest just because . . . well just because we can.

Other than the fact that they cost less and are available in places where broadband lines sometimes can't reach, it's hard to justify keeping a dial-up modem around—unless you're the kind of person who believes something can only be good if you have to wait for it. Waiting was the name of the game for anyone using modems in the early days of the Web. Keeping your sanity meant keeping a magazine or some knitting within close range of the computer at all times.

But for most of us, slow connections and the noises of the modem elicit memories of a time when the Web wasn't so integral to every part of life—it was something the lucky few had but didn't necessarily need. You could afford to wait. It was for playing and exploring and communicating in small doses that were billable by the minute. The modem's little song could set off a Pavlovian reaction, triggering increases in dopamine just because of everything that our Internet time stood for.

When all systems were go—the modem successfully made its connection, no one had been waken up, and you finally got online—there was a sense of accomplishment that left you hopeful, relieved, and even a little proud. The closest equivalent today might be the ritual of searching for, and then connecting to, that one bar of an unlocked wireless network that can only be accessed when your laptop is atop the fridge. But it's not really the same.

DICTIONARIES

Hefty reference books filled with a comprehensive collection of alphabetized words that could—nay, would—yield the great American novel, if only you could figure out what order to put them in.

•   •   •

"Let's look it up!" were words trilled for generations by parents in homes populated by children who had yet to learn that a trip to the dictionary was inevitable once they dared ask "What does that mean?" As a mom or dad, you were well aware that the phrase could parlay any pesky question into a learning opportunity, without betraying the fact that you didn't actually know the answer yourself.

Dictionaries often seemed a nuisance to children. "How do I look it up if I don't know how to spell it?" was an oft heard refrain in classrooms. But the notched, featherweight pages were treasured by anyone who harbored a love of words or a crossword puzzle habit.

A taste for the books' delights would likely grow with age: By high school, many a teen would discover that starting an introductory paragraph in an essay by quoting the definition of a word ("According to *Merriam-Webster's Collegiate Dictionary*, 'unoriginal' is defined as . . .") would get them at least one sentence closer to finishing a research paper.

But dictionary sales have been declining steeply since 2004, dropping by as much as 50 percent in England. A direct result of the decreased use of dictionaries is, arguably, our diminished ability to spell. The constant referencing of difficult words led to generations of decent spellers who knew that memorizing how many Cs and Ms there were in "accommodate" could save a trip to the bookshelf. Typewriters had no squiggly red lines that popped up to indicate faults. Letters and memos and school papers would have to be completely retyped if there wasn't a decent Webster's nearby, leading you to check the spelling of a word even if you were pretty certain of it, just to make sure. In present times, however, there is little shame in announcing that you are a challenged speller. In 2008, the Spelling Society, a British organization, found that out of a thousand people, less than half could correctly spell the words "millennium" and "embarrassed."

Unlike automatic spell-checks in modern computer programs, dictionaries offered up complete definitions for each word, which was a more edifying experience than right-clicking in Microsoft Word in order to deduce a word's meaning by its synonyms. What's more, the big books could lure you in to discovering new words adjacent to the one you wanted—a form of vocabulary expansion that predated the Word-a-Day e-mails that keep getting caught in your spam filter. A desktop widget or iPhone dictionary might be convenient, but the difficulty of browsing through its words has made the "Dictionary" parlor game—stumping partygoers by making up definitions for uncommon words—nearly impossible without just typing in some random letters and hoping that an unusual word will materialize.

Mindlessly flipping through the pages of a dictionary could even, constitute a form of quiet entertainment—especially for those who collected older dictionaries that had yet to take on a more modern, objective tone. Readers of the first English dictionary of note, written by Samuel Johnson in 1755, would've found "orgasm" defined as "sudden vehemence," and "oats" as "a grain, which in England is generally given to horses, but in Scotland supports the people."

One sorry result of the migration of dictionaries to the online realm is the downsizing of books that once aimed for comprehensiveness. Because of printing costs and publishers' desires to cater to consumers who want reference books to be streamlined and utilitarian, some words are staring into their graves. In 2008, Great Britain's *Collins English Dictionary* announced the proposed suspension of several dozen words they'd deemed obsolete, including "agrestic" (rural), "olid" (foul-smelling), and "skirr" (a whirring sound). Meanwhile, the *Oxford Junior Dictionary* recently removed words that were comparatively quotidian in order to shrink the size of the tome while still making room for a few terms they felt would be more relevant to modern children's lives, like "MP3 player" and "voicemail." The edition is made for children and isn't meant to be all-inclusive, but the paring down of words suggests a decreased chance that kids will discover new and useful terms by just idly flipping through the big book. "Ox," "tulip," "goblin," "duke," "holly," and "lobster" are among the hundred-plus words that the Oxford publishers have axed, as is one that old Johnson would've been particularly sad to see go: "oats."

DIRECTORY ASSISTANCE

A telephone information line used to find local businesses and residences; reached by dialing 411 or 555-1212 and manned by voice recognition robots and/or operators; often required that callers have the ability and patience to repeatedly spell the names of provinces such as "Boston" and "Florida." Eventually only used by anyone who'd lost a cell phone, and lacked Internet access, and still had a home phone, and was in desperate need of a pizza.

DITTO PAPER

Sheet coated with a solvent when it went around the drum of a crank-operated machine; the solvent dissolved enough of the pigment on a wax-treated master sheet to create a duplicate without using ink; often found at churches and schools populated with people obsessed with sniffing paper.

DOING NOTHING AT WORK

A vegetative state entered by office workers who did not have actual work to do at their jobs.

• • •

In the 1999 film *Office Space,* the main character, Peter Gibbons, is frank when his superiors ask him to describe his average day. "I generally come in at least fifteen minutes late. I use the side door," he says, "and after that I just sorta space out for about an hour. I just stare at my desk; but it looks like I'm working. I do that for probably another hour after lunch, too. I'd say in a given week I probably only do about fifteen minutes of real, actual work." This admission leads to a promotion.

The twentieth century's best minds brought us many wonders fantastic (Decaf soy lattes! M16s! Plastic!), but what is truly stunning is the number of office hours Americans clocked during those same years doing . . . nothing much. Healthy employment rates meant that there were sometimes surpluses of jobs. There were also many more positions than there are today that required little brain power; these menial and rote tasks can now largely be done by nonhumans (or non-Americans). To the office drone who was waiting for a call to come through so that it could be transferred or alphabetizing a file hidden within a file, taking a cigarette break could sometimes nudge time to move a little faster. The water cooler was also created for this purpose. But in those many empty moments between tasks, much time was spent staring into space, contemplating the moment when the little hand would reach the quitting hour, and life could start up again. This meant that we had to develop ways of balancing our heads just so, in order to ensure that, from the back, we appeared to be awake; it meant drinking at lunch; it meant resigning ourselves to the idea that we had to hand over the hours between nine and five in order to have autonomy between five and nine.

In some professions, downtime was practically a requirement of the job, and higher-ups would charge underlings with figuring out how to use it.

"When I started in the early 80s, there were word-processing centers," recalls attorney Howard Gutman, a partner at Williams & Connolly, a law firm in Washington, DC. "A 120-page brief could take two hours, and one mistake, and you'd have to do it over again. Printing places would vie for business by having beds and food. If you were a young lawyer, sitting and waiting there really was your job."

In the heady days when employment was high and companies kept jobs in America, doing nothing was often far from a punishable fault. It was almost a badge of honor: a refusal to relinquish individuality or kowtow to the Man. Yes, you had to work, but, no, you didn't really have to *be* there. Indeed, if you showed yourself to be fully present, bad things could happen. What good did job devotion do for Willy Loman? When Frank Wheeler, the antihero of Richard Yates's 1961 novel, *Revolutionary Road*, gets so fed up with doing nothing that he invests just a modicum of effort into his job, it starts him down a path that spits him into a tragic existence in which he plays the part of one of the gray-flannel-suit-workaday men he'd always detested.

With the advent of computers, however, the cubicle dweller suddenly received an arsenal of new tools for combating workday ennui—and, by proxy, engaging the brain. There came to seem like less of a need to whitewash the mind in order to get through the average day. Historians have yet to fully realize the effect that pre-loaded computer games like Minesweeper had on the country's national output—its debut and the decrease in this country's production of paperclip chains is hard to overlook. Sadly, it was a form of doing nothing that suspiciously resembled work: Locate problem! Avoid problem! Make vapid smiley faces!

Free time was further threatened when employers began cutting jobs and pushing for increases in worker productivity. But idle time's true death knell was the Internet, which created a way to fill every moment while giving the appearance of business. The joys of making wastebasket two-pointers and using Scotch tape to extract nasal blackheads pale when compared to the minute-hand-massaging possibilities of Craigslist and YouTube. Any employee bivouacking at a reception desk is more likely to be working on a blog or selling lanyards on Etsy than she is to be staring into the ether, counting the number of dots in the foamboard ceiling. According to a Vault.com survey of over 1,100 employees, 90 percent of workers admit that some part of their day is spent doing non-work-related Internet browsing. But more than half of the respondents argued that spending those idle minutes online throughout the day actually made them more productive, thereby shrinking the amount of true do-nothing time spent on the clock.

We remain thankful, however, that our glaze-eyed predecessors were so good at finding ways to occupy themselves as they waited for those workdays to end—after all, many of today's workers would never have come into existence to begin with if their parents hadn't been quite so desperate to pass the time.

DYING OF OLD AGE

Termination of life attributed to no specific failing or occurrence other than senescence and overexposure to *Wheel of Fortune*. Common when a vast majority of US deaths occurred outside of hospitals.

EASY-TO-OPEN PACKAGING

Product encasements that required little effort to open and didn't upstage their contents.

• • •

Thanks to the fact that merchandise is sold in containers that increasingly require a box cutter, a kitchen knife, scissors, or pure brute strength in order to be opened, packaging has evolved to the point where it has lost its charm, even for children who often delighted more in a box than in its contents. Gifts exchanged in public usually need to be brought home before they can be plied open, inspected, and enjoyed; children can't trot out of a store holding a new doll without first dislodging it from a prison of wires and plastic force fields. Indeed, we can no longer go straight from purchasing something to using it: There now is an interim step that renders every purchase potentially dangerous. According to the US Consumer Product Safety Commission, in 2004 more than six thousand people were sent to emergency rooms because of injuries incurred while trying to open packages.

Made from multiple layers of stiff thermoplastic polymer, "clamshell" packages have provided a way for consumers to get a full view of a product and all its accessories before bringing it to the register. Usually the casings are molded to create a bubble over a product (or to conform to the product's shape) and then sealed all the way around. They're largely a response to a market that craves devices that are tiny—if small things like flash drives and SIM cards and MP3 players are encased in bulbous packaging, they become much harder to steal. Companies also like to employ stiff, sculpted packaging because it keeps an appliance or toy's many pieces in place so that things don't shift around or break or spill out during their long journey from Santa's Workshop (a.k.a. China).

Designer Wendy Jedlicka traces the beginning of the complicated-packaging movement to the 1980s, when warehouse stores began to hit the mainstream. "In those huge stores, there's a lot of shelf space, but not so many employees," she says. "The packaging both has to sell the product and protect it from theft because there aren't salespeople around to do all that." The result, however, is that packaging, once something that could be thrown to the side and hardly noticed, has become a major obstacle for consumers.

The problem has exploded to the point that *Consumer Reports* has started issuing an annual tongue-in-cheek "Oyster Award" for the worst package designs. In response to the issue, several companies have released tools especially designed to open plastic clamshells. These tools, thankfully, usually come sans packaging. Many stores, however, don't carry them, although it's unclear whether this is because retailers are trying not to draw attention to the fact that their products require a degree in engineering in order to be liberated, or because their lack of a hard force field makes them so attractive to thieves.

EATING FOR PLEASURE

The practice of not obsessing about food.

• • •

Today, it takes little strain for middle-class Americans to feed their families. Like so many things that are long coveted, once food became cheap and easily accessible, we changed our perspective on it—we became suspicious.

Is it vegan? Gluten-free? Organic? Would a French woman eat it? We've discovered our inner nutritionists, defining ourselves by what we can and can't eat, should and shouldn't eat, do and don't eat, and, in doing so, we've turned dieting and food scrutinizing into a national concern. We seesaw between extremes, either over-analyzing our diets or berating ourselves for finishing an entire pint of Chubby Hubby in one sitting.

Which is the better way to be? It's hard to say. If you eat the bare minimum number of calories per day, research shows that you could extend your life expectancy by decades, or you could just be hungry all the time; eat nothing and you could become a runway model, or you could become dead; consume sixty-six hot dogs in twelve minutes and you could become famous on Coney Island! Or just really sick. Either way, it's become hard to let your kid indulge in the after-school ritual of, say, biting into a deli cookie—the kind that's bigger than your face—without worrying about the trans fats that might lie therein, or the landfill into which its cellophane wrapper will soon land, or the guilt you'll feel when your child is old enough to obsessively calculate his own body mass index.

In several states, strict regulation of the sugar content of food that's allowed inside of public schools means that some children will never know what it is to have cupcakes in the classroom on someone's birthday, or to pick out the M&M's from the otherwise not-so-good cookies offered up at bake sales in the gym. It's become almost unimaginable to think back on that innocent time not so long ago when steak was an everyday breakfast food and the phrase "running off dessert" evoked little more than maybe the thought of a car fueled by Bosco.

We didn't end up in this place overnight. The last half of the twentieth century was a time full of mixed feelings about food. The 1950s and 60s brought us TV dinners and an influx of fast-food restaurants; the pendulum swung in the other direction in the 70s, when words like "organic" and "vegetarian" caught on. Then we hit the era of exercise fanaticism and the Slim Fast diet—in the 80s and 90s, no sitcom was complete without a teen facing an eating disorder. Even Garfield was a chronic dieter. But it was also the height of the Happy Meal and the sugar-filled juice box.

Now, we're busy either congratulating ourselves for eating only Community Supported Agriculture–purchased greens washed down with homemade kombucha, or else we're promising ourselves that tomorrow we'll start the Master Cleanse diet to wash away our nutritional sins. Knowing the fat content of every Big Mac we consume might be making us healthier, but it's also making us stressed. And the thing about stress is that it has the power to make a bag of chips magically disappear.

Sara Moulton, *Gourmet* magazine's longtime executive chef, has watched wholesomeness challenge convenience—while pleasure sits on the bench.

"It's gotten to an extreme, and I could do without the snobbishness. At the end of the day, food should be fun and tasty and that's what matters more than anything else," she says. "The plus side of the so called 'locavore' movement—getting food from local sources—is that that food tastes better because it's not being grown with the purpose of holding up during shipping, it's being grown for taste and not sturdiness. But a side effect is that it's made some people view food as a religion, which is ridiculous. Food is first and foremost there to nurture us. It should never be this intellectual, psychological, crazy thing. To get so obsessed about where each thing on your plate came from and what's in season—it's admirable but it's also elitist." Indeed, the poorest people in this country are also the most obese, largely because they can't afford to shop at a local farmers' market or Whole Foods. They're instead trying to get enjoyment from fast-food burgers, "which, to be honest, don't taste as good as they used to if they're not made with trans fats!" Ms. Moulton says. "So on the one hand, you have the elitists who are worshiping their food instead of enjoying it—those who just assume that because something is organic it automatically means it'll taste better—and on the other you have those who are craving sugars and salts and fatty things because it's what they're used to and what they can afford."

Awareness about calories, meanwhile, may help our waistlines, but it's made every bite feel extra loaded. In the 90s, the FDA began to require that packaged food have its nutritional value stamped on its side, waving in the era of the obsessive calorie counter; no longer would it be possible to fully enjoy a Hostess cupcake without first removing your reading glasses. By the 2000s, even Cookie Monster was preaching that cookies are just a "sometimes" food. Then again, Cookie Monster never actually swallowed his food to begin with.

Talk about problems.

ENCYCLOPEDIAS

Big books that acted as CliffsNotes to science, history, people, and life on Earth as we knew it.

• • •

For generations, door-to-door salesmen and infomercial-makers banked on the fact that the world's mothers and fathers and grandparents would not be averse to spending heartily on yards of encyclopedias, if only because such a phalanx of books served as visual proof that they cared about educating the next generation. Did the volumes grow dusty on high-up shelves? Sometimes. Were they frequently used as flower presses and stepstools? Perhaps. Still, proud families displayed their collections and hoped that their children might get lost in the books that somehow managed to package up all the world's knowledge so neatly. No matter how many Cheetos you let your children eat, or how many hours of Duck Hunt you allowed them to play, you could at least know that you'd given them the opportunity for advancement, even if they didn't take it: It was a form of betterment-by-vicinity, not unlike putting a Bible on a motel nightstand.

When research reports were due, the utility of having an authoritative guide to everything in the world just a few feet down from mom's collection of V.C. Andrews books suddenly became invaluable. There was also the fact that a teacher couldn't possibly have the same set as every one of his students, which meant that the books became excellent tools for cribbing.

Today, however, Google and Wikipedia and all their unverified sources have been handed the authority that once belonged only to the likes of *Britannica*. The encyclopedia industry began feeling the heat of the digital revolution in the 1990s, but information packed and sold on CDs and DVDs—then the medium's main competition—lacked the same kind of physical heft. The new formats also changed the way in which you could trot through history: Calling up an entry on a screen deprived you of the kind of unexpected ambling that you could do while flipping randomly through those featherweight pages. It also deprived you of artillery should your studying be interrupted by a rat.

As information steadily becomes decreasingly tangible, encyclopedias are enriching little more than landfill soil. The Internet is largely quashing the need for multivolume print encyclopedias, but this has led to a new question converse to the one posed by encyclopedia usage: Instead of asking if it's wise to rely on just one source, you instead find yourself wondering which of a million sources can possibly be trusted. The most seemingly trustworthy ones can often be the dullest to read, making the leather-bound tomes of your childhood seem comparatively lively. Thanks to Wikipedia's myriad of self-appointed, nameless editors' efforts to keep everything objective and trustworthy, the entries often lack anything near the prose and insight that was found in the big books' old bylined entries, so often packed with unexpected points-of-view and stamped with the omnipotent publisher's golden seal of approval.

Wikipedia has, however, added a new twist to the research experience, allowing you the opportunity to add your own entries and to annotate ones that already exist. Old fashioned paper reference books didn't let you feel quite so important. If *Britannica* cared what you thought, they'd call.

EVENING NEWS

Television programs that were often watched by families en groupe; formerly considered Must-See TV; says former Secretary of State

Madeleine Albright: "Network nightly news broadcasts were a source of common information and national unity. Opinions differed, but Americans began thinking with the same images and facts in mind, brought to them by experienced journalists. If you cared about national or world affairs, you scheduled dinner before or after the nightly serving of Cronkite, Rather, Brokaw, or Jennings."

EXECUTIVE CHAIRS

Status symbols on wheels.

• • •

Kings sat on big thrones, so why shouldn't the head of accounting? Such was the rationale that dictated seat choices of office higher-ups for decades. Small chairs were set aside for more plebian toilers who had not yet reached the acme of success at which they were granted the great privilege of picking out their own office furniture.

However there was something fundamentally illogical about this system of seat stratification: The padded, high-backed "executive" chairs looked impressive and were cozy to luxuriate in, but they actually weren't that comfortable if you had sit for long periods. Paradoxically, these trophy chairs were generally rather cheap to produce (the key ingredient was inexpensive foam). The "task" chairs used by the worker bees—harder seats that were generally better for your back—were usually more complex structures that could be customized to fit people of various sizes and shapes, yet their many adjustable aspects made it hard to pare down production costs. They also weren't interesting to look at, no matter how artfully the surrounding cubicle was decorated.

So there was big and small, and little in between. Goldilocks would've been at quite a loss . . . unless she was office trawling during the late 90s. Then she might've found herself in a seat that was *just* right: the 1994 Aeron chair by Herman Miller, a piece of industrial furniture that revolutionized the way we thought about office seating.

Because of the proliferation of computers, people were sitting at their desks in fixed positions for longer periods of time than ever before. Offices were also becoming normal parts of people's homes, creating a need for a chair that you'd want to enjoy outside of the cubicle; values were starting to shift so that bigger didn't always mean better. Instead, the smaller something was, the more status it might represent—whether it be a computer, a phone, or a person (this was the Kate Moss era, after all).

The Aeron, which came in a revolutionary three sizes, was something completely different. Before it, office chairs had arms that usually attached to the seat. The Aeron's attached to the back, making them more adjustable. The chair butterflied at the top to better support the shoulders. The position of the seat and back of the chair supported the natural forward tilt of the pelvis to give the spine its proper S-curve, which would appeal to increasingly health-conscious execs. Its internal structure wasn't hidden; it lacked upholstery altogether. Unlike its predecessors, it was expensive to produce. Like its predecessors, it had a big price tag: over $800 when it first hit the market.

What's not to love about such an innovative chair? Apparently, if the company had listened to the marketing department, almost everything. "The initial reaction from the marketing people was: You can't sell a chair without upholstery," says industrial designer Don Chadwick, who codesigned the chair. "The expectation was always that the big chairs were more comfortable, but we proved that you can have a much more comfortable chair with far less material." Nevertheless, the chair went on to redefine a genre, spawning a million copycats and landing behind nearly any desk that mattered. The fact that it became part of the Museum of Modern Art's permanent collection of design even before it was available to the public made it seem all the more suited to eminence. It wasn't just a rear support system . . . it was *ahhht*.

And that fancy, old, leather behemoth? Maybe the intern could use it.

FARM STUDS

Unneutered farm animals who made sweet love when and how they pleased; now largely replaced by turkey basters loaded with mail-order semen.

FAX MACHINES

E-mail predecessors used to transmit documents over long distances.

• • •

Sometimes the only way to officially prove that you are actually, really, and truly the person you say you are is to sign your name in pen and ink—and this doesn't work so well when you try to do it on an LCD screen. Yes, there are plenty of ways to approve online transactions, but physical John Hancocks are still often the only things people trust. So, until we grow arms that are long enough to reach and put a non-pixilated signature on printed documents that we've e-mailed across the country, we'll probably have to tolerate fax machines or some version of them—even if they're woefully past their prime.

Facsimile technology has been around in one incarnation or another for more than 150 years, and the technology behind it has changed very little. The general process of conveying images using telegraph lines, electric currents, pendulums, and steadily-rotating cylinders is what was responsible for sending facsimiles for the bulk of the device's lifetime. The first faxes, much like today's, broke an image down to a series of tiny squares and then discerned—and conveyed—whether or not each of those miniscule areas was light or dark. In the 1970s, when they were known as telecopiers, the drums whirled around in plain view under a Plexiglas lid, with a stylus etching out the image using back-and-forth strokes. The whole process took at least five minutes per page, and required the use of chemically treated paper wrapped onto spools. Heat was used to burnish dark areas, but the resulting images weren't meant to last: eventually natural light would cause the paper to turn dark or yellow. It wasn't until the late 80s that there was at last the proliferation of faxes that took real paper instead of spools of the shiny heat-activated stuff that you needed three paperweights and a coffee mug to hold flat.

At the height of their popularity in the 80s and 90s, faxes were found in every office and in many homes. When they weren't being utilized for work purposes, they were sometimes used as precursors to e-mail: People sent correspondence to family members living abroad, or forwarded frightening (and false) warnings about children's stickers laced with acid and gangs who drove around with their lights off at night (the quality of the images of these viral hoaxes, which were made to look like they'd been copied from police reports, often deteriorated with each fax, but this somehow made them look all the more valid).

But e-mail and scanners have rendered faxes mostly useless—and the less we use them, the worse we get at manipulating the little monsters, often resorting to prayers to the Fax God. It's a machine that requires a degree of humility. Hook, dial! Or is it dial, hook? Call! Wait, do you need to press call? Maybe you should pick up the phone that's attached to the thing. It'll be fine as long as you insert paper faceup. No, facedown. Why did it start feeding before the paper was even in? Now it's beeping! That's good. Or is it? In the end, you just press the green start button and hope for the best . . .

Paper lovers can take solace in the fact that Internet faxes have caught on enough to bridge the divide between digital and paper-and-ink communications, attracting some of the people who are still wary of sending personal information over the Internet, despite the fact that they still hand their credit cards to strangers in stores willy-nilly.

The capricious machines can still be found in many offices, gathering piles of unclaimed sheets of paper at their bases. Maybe, just maybe, one of those pages will be a confirmation sheet (a throwback to a time when it was acceptable to use an entire piece of paper just to convey one sentence saying "yea" or "nay"). Or maybe they've just been burping out offers for home refinancing packages, or cruises to the Bahamas, or completely black pages sent by pranksters intent on sucking all the ink out of the huffing-and-puffing old appliance. For shame.

FILM

Thin strips of plastic covered with light-sensitive chemicals, used to create prints of images that could be found on mantels, tucked inside wallets, and on casting agents' floors.

• • •

Before the advent of digital cameras, photography was a kind of waiting game. In the 1820s—the very earliest days of photography—it meant waiting eight hours to expose film in order to get just one photo; in later decades, the Daguerreotype process sped things up, but exposures could still be as long as fifteen minutes. Around the turn of the century, the newly formed Eastman Kodak company released the Brownie, a camera that was portable and didn't require lengthy exposure time. Still, people had to ship the whole camera back to Kodak and then wait for their photos to arrive in the mail. We did this take-the-pictures-then-wait-for-development dance for the better part of a century.

Photographers and high-school art class students often developed their own film in darkrooms, but your average amateur photographer dropped off her film at a pharmacy's photo department or sent it to a prints-by-mail service. If you were willing to pay a premium, you could take it to a one-hour-photo place. Either way, some photo-tech elf mixed together just the right amount of chemicals to transform your strip of 35mm-wide film into something that would spend the rest of its lifetime in a shoebox under your bed.

Once the prints were in hand (where they were carefully cradled, lest you leave fingerprints), you'd cringe at unflattering shots. At least you'd gotten a shot at all—entire museums could be filled with the world's photos of blurry fingers and lens caps. But a bad photo of yourself could be crushing. Your shiny forehead reflecting the flash, your

eyes red, your stomach hanging over your jeans . . . Did you look like that all the time? In the digital age, these kinds of images are just erased, and you can quickly forget ever seeing yourself in such an unfortunate pose. Then, however, you ripped up the offending images. Or maybe you stuffed them in that shoebox, somehow knowing that one day you'd think they really weren't so bad, if only because you'd gotten so much fatter in the interim.

But you never really knew what you'd find once you pried open the envelope's sticky flap to reveal that stack of twenty-four or thirty-six prints—or forty-eight or seventy-two if you asked for doubles. Would the photos even be yours? Embarrassing shots were extra-special once you remembered that the pharmacy employees had likely already seen them. There was often the disappointment of what was absent from those envelopes when they finally did come—a photo that you could've sworn you'd taken, or a person's head. (There was no LCD screen showing the image back then. You had to judge what was in the frame by using one eye and a one-centimeter view finder.)

Once you snapped the shutter, an image was irreversibly exposed to the film. This meant that you were constantly asking yourself if something was really photo-worthy. Do you take pictures in the Louvre, or just buy postcards so that there'll be shots left over for that evening walk on the Seine? Will nighttime photos even come out? Should you use a flash? 200-speed film or 400? Are you really going to want to remember what this guy looks like naked? These were calculations that even an amateur photographer had to make.

Other times you'd go snap-happy. After gleefully taking pictures of just about anything, you'd notice a big fat zero in the "pictures remaining" dial. Note to self: It's hard to get good shots if you don't have film in the camera.

The demand for film fell along with the rise of digital photography in the late 1990s. With unlimited shots, instant gratification, and convenient photo storage, digital cameras set the new standard in photography. One of their many draws was that they made photos a lot easier to share and copy, which meant that there were fewer people handing their camera to the one sorry soul charged with taking the group picture at the holiday party while everyone said, "Cheese!" And then "Cheese!" And then "Cheese!"

By 2003, digital camera sales had surpassed those of film cameras, leaving little use for film cartridges. Digital made photography faster and easier, but also a little less precious. The fewer schools that build darkrooms and teach the chemistry of photography, the fewer kids will grow up to know what it is to have to set fire to a really bad picture, and the fewer youngsters will dream of one day working at the CVS one-hour-photo counter. But you'll likely hold onto some of the little black plastic film containers, putting baby teeth or marijuana in the spot that used to hold a tiny canister of hope.

FOCUS GROUPS

Collection of average citizens who were gathered together—and paid—to discuss their thoughts on a project or idea that a company was testing. Was nice work if you could get it. Says marketing guru Seth Godin, "They never worked, really. Only the top pros understood them. Mostly, they were used to persuade the boss to do what you wanted to do anyway. Now, a focus group is known as a blog."

FULL WORDS

Combinations of consonants and vowels combined to make words that were then paired with other nouns, verbs, articles, et al, in order to produce comprehensible subjects and predicates.

• • •

Today's documenter of modern life can be found hunched over a cell phone in a crowded subway trying to squeeze as much emotion and information as possible into a screen that only allows 160 characters. His tool is a keyboard that has a mere twelve buttons that require at least five pushes just to summon up a capital S. How can prose possibly blossom in such confines?

Easily. A little surgery is all that is required to make long words into easily thumb-able rebuses. Why take the extra time and work and space to write out a full explanation to someone when you're already 5 mn l8? Why press ten buttons when you can convey the same idea with four? Energy must be conserved if one expects to keep up with the dozens of conversations that can go on at the same time via cell phones without ever actually having to talk. The proliferation of phones that have full keyboards have made us even faster; T9, a feature that guessed which letter you were about to type in order to ease the burden of writing full words on twelve buttons, seems in and of itself outdated. Written communication might just be the ultimate winner of the technological revolution: According to Gartner, a company that tracks the growth of the mobile phone industry, there are currently more than a trillion text messages sent a year. The loser? English as we knew it.

But that might not be such a bad thing.

Today, we relay messages with such fluency that it's hard to remember that not long ago so many of us—especially people who are actually paid to write—would seize up when trying to jot a note to the cleaning person. There was handwriting to consider, not to mention spelling and word choice. It's a process that today would seem foreign to the average texter or e-mailer, who no longer recites the "I before E" poem or runs to the dictionary in order to verify a spelling. Writing something out phonetically will do the job. Apostrophes are rarely necessary, words have been truncated, and new acronyms invented.

Of course, languages are always in a constant state of flux. English has evolved in ways that have made things easier for us. Adding an "-ed" to some verbs would've probably seemed very lazy to Milton or Chaucer. "Climb" was once "clomb." "Treaded" used to be less favorable than "trod." And when was the last time anyone "rent" open a bag of pretzels? There's also a long tradition of word-truncation from the development of Morse Code in the 1830s to the invention of the telegram in the

1890s—both forms of communication that put value on the terseness of correspondences. Before typewriters, businessmen frequently wrote to each other using truncated words and agreed-upon symbols in order to save time and ink and to indicate that they were so busy and successful that they didn't have the time to spell out every word.

In his book *TXTNG: The Gr8 Db8*, linguist David Crystal argues that today we have largely embraced texting because we're innately drawn to word play. He also points out the inordinate number of anti-text-messaging articles that have been written largely in text-ese, thanks to writers using the subject matter as an excuse to flex a new muscle. Abbreviations have even slipped into spoken language; few exclamations are as filled with a mix of excitement and irony as an intoned "oh em gee."

But it's undeniable that this kind of manipulation of the language has stirred up unprecedented ire. Shakespeare had permission to create new words, 7th graders—one may argue—do not.

As one grumpy Harvard student wrote in the school's newspaper in 2008: "Text messaging will be the downfall of Western civilization. It's twenty times worse than AIM. Phones are for SPEAKING, not writing. It also gives people an excuse to type and speak even worse than they did before. Pretty soon it spills over into everyday speech, and not only do you want to slam your head in a drawer because of what a person is saying, but because of the way they're saying it too. By the end of this text message movement, we're all going to be hooting and yelling like monkeys and banging the phones in much the same way, except we'll have good hair and a pair of Asics."

GAS STATION ATTENDANTS

Jump-suited service station employees who pumped fuel, wiped windshields, and checked the oil of cars, before it was discovered that most people (namely, those outside of New Jersey and Oregon) don't mind pumping their own gas and will do it for free.

GETTING LOST

An occurrence whereby one loses an object, a person, or their sense of direction.

. . .

In 1983, President Reagan decreed that global positioning systems, theretofore the provenance of the military, would be opened up to the public. Little did the Gipper know how this decision would affect the lives of so many couples who'd grown accustomed to being deadlocked on whether or not to ask for directions. It'd lead to fewer people handing the phone to someone better at giving directions, or suggesting navigation tips based on the distance to a Bob's Big Boy. There would also be a serious dip in the number of cartographer wannabes mapping out entire highways on a square cocktail napkin.

In an era where "MapQuest" is a verb, having no sense of direction or lacking the ability to read an atlas have become excusable flaws. Handheld GPS devices, now mostly used in cars and cell phones, are even helping people keep an eye on the locations of kids, impaired adults, and pets. Technology-focused market research company Forward Concepts estimates that by 2011, there will be 520 million shipments of GPS units made worldwide—nearly five times as many as in 2006.

But if life truly is about the journey and not the destination, losing "lost" could be a real loss. Consider the ramifications on Western culture had the technology popped up sooner. Would there be an *Odyssey*? Columbus might've actually found the Orient ("Make the next legal U-Turn").

Getting lost is a phenomenon that is fading in realms outside the world of cars and roads. In a world obsessed with control and information hoarding, people seem to worry more about "finding themselves" in something than "losing themselves" in anything. The very word is in danger of becoming a linguistic remnant as nonsensical as "dialing" a phone that has buttons. There may always be those intangible losses—minds, loves, innocence—but today most visual memories are saved on hard drives, and if you pay the right person the right amount of money, he will likely find that computer file you thought was permanently missing. Objects that once regularly had you praying to St. Anthony—Keys! Phones! Wallets! Birth control!—can now can be equipped with doodads that'll chirp when called.

Part of the issue is the fact that things have become so replaceable that losses are no longer as noticeable—an indication that perhaps sentimentality is also on the decline. A copy of a first-edition book you misplaced is there for the taking on eBay; an Old Navy sock that lost its partner in Memphis can likely pick up a replacement stuck to a dryer at a Laundromat in Trenton or Fresno. Even losing a wallet is a hardship that can be mollified by a quick call to the credit card company, which can replace the cards and may even make up for the cash and the cost of the missing wallet. If Ella Fitzgerald lost her little yellow basket today, she'd need only alert American Express.

Losing touch is also soon to be as old fashioned an idea as pulling out a map that would be helpful if you only knew which way was north. There are sites that can make it easy to find people you regret losing—thanks to Craigslist's Missed Connections, a cute guy you met at a bar weeks ago can be located even if you lost his number. But having a leash on everyone you've ever met isn't always a blessing. On social-networking sites, a high-school lab partner you haven't thought about in a decade may suddenly start notifying you every time he posts a photo online, oblivious to the fact that you were quite happy only having to deal with him at reunions once or twice a decade. It can also be a liability in situations where eventual anonymity seemed a blessing: Spring-breakers who once paired off with the impunity that comes with knowing that you'll never see someone again now have to deal with the reality that they may be Googled by their beachside paramour for years to come. Indeed, Google searches of old friends and lovers have ripped away the romance of spontaneously reuniting with someone you thought was lost to you forever.

But losing sight of our meandering ways and the connections made with people during unexpected sojourns may be the biggest loss of all. That, and the ability to formulate snide answers to that pervasive childhood question that today's kids are better off addressing to the little Mr. T or Kathleen Turner living inside the GPS: "Are we there yet?"

GIRDLES

Elasticized undergarments that made the wearer look sexy, eliminating the need to diet, exercise, or marry a surgeon. Those who relied heavily on girdles during the day also relied on very dark rooms at night.

HANDKERCHIEFS

Small, square reusable pieces of fabric used for blowing one's nose; reinserted into pocket or purse after use. Fell out of favor once it was generally understood that this is a completely disgusting thing to do.

HD-DVDS

Short for High Definition Digital Versatile Discs. A DVD successor that could hold a greater amount of information and reveal more definition and crisper images than earlier formats. Although the format, which was launched in 2005, was backed by Toshiba and had its diehard fans, Blockbuster and major motion picture studios ended up deciding to release films in Blu-ray instead, a format that, although more expensive, made every pixilated nose's clogged pores all the more lifelike. HD-DVDs were discontinued in 2008. Reminiscent of the Betamax/VHS battle of the 1980s (see Videos).

HIGH-DIVING BOARDS

Three-meter poolside springboards; a legal way to get high.

• • •

Sissy! Wimp! Dingleberry! Those were the words you knew you'd hear if you decided to turn around and scoot down the diving board's ladder. After all, you'd only just reached the top of that same ladder, working up courage with each slippery step as the slicked heads below you got smaller. You padded your way to the tip of the sandpapery precipice, balancing as the board bounced with every step. When you reached the edge, you suddenly felt a new appreciation for the size of a meter: just three of them stacked one atop the other was awfully high. But hey, if there was really that much risk involved, they wouldn't allow people on the diving board to begin with . . . right? Still, maybe you should've waited a little longer after eating, or worn a less wedgie-prone bathing suit. And didn't it seem like that swimmer down there was a little too close to where you were going to land? Beneath you, the older kids grew visibly impatient. If you knew exactly which epithets were about to be tossed your way, it was only because you'd been yelling them at someone else just minutes earlier. Who knew a public pool could feel so much like death row?

Maybe you just took one timid step off the edge. Maybe you jumped, or did a jackknife. A belly flop would hurt like a mother and certainly wasn't going to impress anyone, but it'd rank you slightly higher than the kids who never attempted to climb the board at all. Those who dared to actually dive off the board earned the real seats of honor in the pool hierarchy.

"It was just such an adrenaline rush. Yes, there was risk, but it was a reasonable amount of risk—and lots of things are only fun because it feels like there's some danger involved," says Greg Munro, a Montana law professor who spent most of his childhood summers hanging out around the diving board in Missoula. As an adult, he wanted to see if he still had what it took to dive off the end of a three-meter board, but he couldn't find anywhere to test out his latent skills: the high-diving boards, and even most of the low ones, had been yanked out of all the local public pools.

What went wrong in the equation? The physics of diving hadn't changed. People still flock to pools come Memorial Day. Kids are as drawn to risk as they ever were.

Perhaps today's coddling parents see their children as less disposable than tots of previous generations? After all, if anything were to happen to the kids, they'd have no excuse to keep the Wii.

The most likely explanation, however, is that insurance companies started to reconsider the wisdom of letting children propel themselves off of ten-foot-high platforms. Of course, pools have never been places known for their safety records. They're slippery. They're deep. They're full of urine and germs and blindfolded children haranguing someone named Marco. Anyone willing to brave such conditions clearly has an appetite for danger. Could diving boards really be more dangerous than, say, the poolside sin known as horseplay?

Maybe. Maybe not. Either way, the diving board industry started to take a plunge in 1993 when the National Spa and Pool Institute was part of a high-profile case where they were sued by a the family of a fourteen-year-old: In attempting to dive in head-first without his arms up for protection, he hit the slope where the pool goes from shallow to deep and became paralyzed from the neck down. His family was awarded $6.6 million, sending the organization into bankruptcy and leading them to remove all stipulations and recommendations regarding the building of diving boards or proper diving techniques. How could they be sued in the future for accidents on boards if they divorced themselves from the diving aspect of pools all together? Insurance companies took note of the big payout, as well as the fact that there was no longer any group setting an industry standard for boards, and they started making it impossible—or at least really expensive—for municipal pool owners and board builders to get the proper insurance.

Industry numbers indicate that diving board sales have dipped by at least 25 percent since the 1990s and are continuing to decline. Many litigation-wary pool builders won't even build a deep end.

That doesn't mean that there are no kids out there perfecting their can-openers—they just aren't doing them off of boards. According to research gathered in the 80s, only 2 percent of all diving accidents happen because of diving boards. The rest occur when people dive from the side of the shallow end of the pool, or off of docks, bridges, or boats. Still, the boards took all the flack.

When he started to realize that there was absolutely no place for him to dive off a high dive, Mr. Munro began examining fifty years of appellate court decisions. He found, on average, just one case a year involving a "serious" diving accident.

"People are rendered quadriplegic in rodeos every day, but it's become easier to find a rodeo than a diving board," says Mr. Munro. "The competitive diving industry, however, has never seen a single death or person rendered paraplegic in a public pool."

Still, few kids today will ever know what it's like to hurl themselves into the deep end from a board. This means you can also wave good-bye to the likelihood that future generations will catch a diving bug so strong that it'll propel them to varsity level and even higher board heights: The US, which won every gold medal in a diving event at the Olympics between 1924 and 1952, has only seen three divers take home a gold since 1980.

HITCHHIKERS

Travelers who bummed rides off of strangers as part of a pre-Craigslist method of ridesharing; see: *It Happened One Night* (Colbert, Claudette), *Even Cowgirls Get The Blues* (Thurman, Uma), and *Pee-Wee's Big Adventure* (Marge, Large).

•   •   •

An opposable thumb is what separates us from our simian ancestors; the way we use it is what separates us from more recent generations. Today, it's rare to see one pointed to the heavens on the side of the road, attached to a young person doing their best to look unthreatening.

Crossroads were once filled with thumbs waving around or bobbing up and down, or kept close to the hip in a manner that broadcasted a kind of laidback brand of cool and experience (veteran thumbers knew that hands kept lower down would be slower to fatigue). They belonged to travelers who were looking for a transportation alternative that promised adventure—gratis. The hitchhiker could even prove useful to the driver: Truckers who traveled long distances sometimes sought them out because having someone to talk to reduced the chances of falling asleep at the wheel. (Good hitchhikers, of course, knew to keep to safe subjects. Sports were usually OK. Sex or politics would likely get you thrown out of the car.) Sometimes, a passenger was there to act as a kind of buffer between arguing spouses. Then there were the times their role was to slash off the driver's head.

Or at least that was the fear. More recently, however, it's become the assumption.

By most accounts, hitchhiking began during the Great Depression, when drivers were generally sympathetic to anyone who was standing on the side of the road clinging to the certainty that employment existed in some other realm just outside of that town or city or state. In the 1960s, hitchhiking saw another surge of popularity, and people started opening up their car doors as quickly as they uncrossed their legs. It was early in that decade that jazz pianist Bill Heid began a hitchhiking career that would eventually take him four hundred thousand miles, through forty-eight states and thirteen countries, looking for old rhythm-and-blues 78s at record stores and visiting baseball stadiums. But mostly, he was just looking for adventure. For seven years, he held *The Guinness Book of Records* title for most miles hitchhiked.

"When you're young, you do that sort of thing for no particular reason," says Mr. Heid, now in his sixties. "I had no fear of death or

lunatics." Among the twenty-one thousand drivers who picked him up during his thirty years on the road were the rock musician Steve Miller, driving a British sports car, and Frankie Yankovic, a.k.a. America's Polka King. Mostly, however, his chauffeurs were solid representatives of middle America: couples bickering about where to stop for gas, old men relishing tales of their war days, and the occasional driver who was a little tipsy and quick to lend him the wheel.

But there was also plenty of downtime. The experienced hitchhiker knew what it was to wait out long fallow periods on the sides of dirt roads where hours seem to pass only occasionally. A slowing car would raise the spirits. A passing one would do the same for your middle finger.

Mr. Heid, however, recalls having pretty good luck with getting rides quickly. His method involved focusing mainly on hailing middle-aged men in nice cars: they were more likely to stop than female drivers, and seemed affluent enough that he didn't think they'd try to steal anything from him. "When I started in the 1960s, I'd go to the turnpike interchange in Monroeville in Pennsylvania near where I grew up, and there'd be over a hundred people there—half of them would be guys from the navy or army, and the rest would be your hippy Joan Baez–type wannabes with their long hair and little dogs," he says. "My method was to wear my little Mr. Goodwrench outfit—a shirt, a necktie—and politely ask people at the crossroads or gas stations if they'd take me. Sometimes I'd make up a little lie and say that I was trying to get to such-and-such a place because I was supposed to shuttle a car from Detroit, or wherever, back to Pittsburgh and I'd missed my ride. I used that more and more as I got older, because it sounded more believable than saying 'I'm in my forties and I don't have a car because I prefer to hitchhike.'"

Through the years, Mr. Heid met his share of people who were quick to lift an eyebrow at anyone who took part in either side of the hitchhiking equation. Some worried that it smelled a little too much like communism. Indeed, there were Eastern Bloc countries that presented hitchhiking coupons to tourists and then gave awards to whichever locals could collect the most of them. There were also many who felt that giving a ride to a stranger was a kind of moral obligation. Religious groups discussed the importance of stopping to help strangers, even if the constant slowing down and speeding up meant paying extra alms to the patron saint of Citgo. In 1978, an eighty-five-year-old minister, Edwin Dahlberg, went so far as to publish a book encouraging good Christians to pick up hitchhikers.

"Nothing is more needed in contemporary society than that we should acquaint ourselves with the causes of people we do not know," he wrote in his tome *I Pick Up Hitchhikers*. "We tend to associate ourselves only with the causes of people we do know . . . Consequently, we live in too small a world." He does, however, acknowledge that it's possible for bad things to happen if you invite strangers into your car, but he uses this point to argue that other seniors in particular should be volunteering their passenger seats with alacrity. "As a fairly ancient senior citizen," he wrote, "it wouldn't make too much difference to the world if [you] did get 'bumped off.'"

With every passing year, however, hitchhiking incidents with bad outcomes became more likely to hit the evening news all around the country. The more the media's focus shifted from local happenings to national news items, the worse the situation got for hitchhikers. There've always been lunatics and misfits and perverts out there, but we didn't used to hear about ones that were far beyond our purview. The serial killer who murdered a half-dozen female hitchhikers off Highway 101 in California in the early 70s also didn't do the pastime any favors. In 1973, *Newsweek* proclaimed that "Instead of the driver fearing the pickup it is now the hitchhiker herself who runs by far the greater risk of being robbed, assaulted, abducted, murdered—or, most likely of all, raped."

Perhaps the largest factor in the demise of hitchhiking is simply the fact that we've come to expect that middle-class families will have at least two cars. With more than one mode of transportation per household, we no longer have to think outside of the box if we want to go to the beach when a spouse or parent or sibling is out running errands.

"I think that if you're a kid today and you go off to college, or even if you're in high school, you more than likely have your own car," says Mr. Heid. "So teens drive themselves or drive each other instead of looking for rides elsewhere." We also get more new cars than we used to, trading in and trading up instead of driving a junker into the ground. This means that it's not just once every decade or two that we go through that new-car stage where we don't want to muss the rubber mats or tarnish that fresh smell by offering the passenger seat to a stranger who might not use Purell.

In a nod to wavering gas prices and an environment that's heavily taxed by the number of cars on the road, rideshares have started to grow in popularity, but they lack the kind of impulsivity and anonymity that hitchhiking offered. They are almost always prearranged online, which means we can exchange names and figure out who is going to bring the iPod adapter long before we meet a prospective passenger. This allows us the ability to Google each other, which removes a degree of anonymity and gives the interaction a veneer of safety. And, perhaps, sterility.

And yet, the same lawmakers who once made it illegal to hitchhike in many states now are encouraging people to pick up roadside passengers during rush hour so that they can drive in HOV lanes which can only be used by cars where there are at least two people. This kind of impromptu carpooling, a practice known as "slugging," has been slow to catch on; another practice, known as putting a blow-up doll in the passenger seat, has gotten a lot more press.

"To be honest," says Mr. Heid, "Even I wouldn't feel safe picking someone up."

HOME ECONOMICS

A course, or entire curriculum, devoted to teaching young women to cook, clean, sew, and educate children, in addition to other essential skills girls would need if they wanted to get that all-important degree: the MRS.

HOTEL KEYS

Metal contraptions given on loan in order to allow access to rented rooms. Often pilfered by travelers.

• • •

Gone are the days of stumbling up from the hotel bar and then spilling out the contents of your pockets or purse in the hotel hallway, your mind woozy from all the martinis that were flowing downstairs. Where is that darn key? Oh, wait—Voilà! The only problem is that it refuses to open the lock, no matter how many choice words you spew. And why does it sound like someone is watching Johnny Carson on the other side of the door? Closer scrutinizing reveals the fact that the number on the fob seems to indicate that your key actually belongs to a lock that's on the door on the other side of the hall. Aha! Eat your heart out, Nancy Drew.

The modern hotel guest is likely not to have such luck when it comes to finding her room, thanks to the fact that most hotels no longer supply key rings that display any kind of number. In fact, few hotels give out keys at all.

Glenn Gould, the pianist, was obsessed with pilfering them, as is Mitchell Wolfson, Jr., founder of Miami's Wolfsonian Museum. His childhood interest in saving hotel keys was, he's said, what inspired him to start many of the collections of odd objects that are now kept in his museum's galleries.

It wasn't hard to be drawn to the little gewgaws, each of which represented a unique experience and time and place. In an online eulogy, Justin Agoglia of Long Island, New York, recalls how his late father, Joseph, was constantly traveling for business and would collect keys from every hotel he visited. He proudly displayed them in the family den. "They were creatively fashioned, and distinct in their colors and shapes. By the time I was a teenager, my father had literally hundreds of keys," writes Mr. Agoglia. "Each key had a story and my father could tell you where he was at the time and the type of trip it was."

But then one day, his father found religion. Apparently, God had a soft spot for Hiltons.

Writes Mr. Agoglia: "As a way of trying to make restitution, [my father] made it a point to identify each key with its respective hotel. And as many as he could identify, he wrote a personal letter explaining what happened and returned the keys."

Of course, the gesture was worth more than the actual keys: by the time he sent them back, most of those hotels had likely replaced all their locks with electric card scanners . . . largely because there were a lot of people out there who weren't as thoughtful as the late Mr. Agoglia. Some tossed the keys altogether. Some copied them. In the 1980s, there was a barrage of charges brought against hotels by former guests who claimed they'd been mugged, robbed, or raped because of faulty key systems. In some cases, the crimes were caused by hotel staffers who had snagged skeleton keys. In other instances, the perpetrators were former guests who had either taken home the room keys or made copies before returning them. Many hotels kept locksmiths on the payroll so that rooms would be regularly rekeyed. Some hotels bought twice as many lock cylinders as they needed, and constantly shuffled them around so that one room wouldn't take the same key two weeks in a row. But there was still the cost of making a new key for the lock and getting a new keychain engraved, and the fact that one misplaced master key would often mean that every lock would have to be completely scrapped.

Also in the 80s, some hotels began switching to punch-card keys— door handles were fitted with card readers that would line up with the holes in the plastic cards; a special card was used to change the formula of holes for each lock after each guest. By the late 90s, nearly all hotels had migrated over to locks that read magnetic strips or computerized chips, much like a credit card reader. These locks were usually at least three times as expensive as the old brass-key-and-deadbolt ones, but they contained microprocessors that had the ability to read millions of combinations. Hotels could hop off the costly and time-consuming rekeying merry-go-round by just generating a new key code for every new check-in. The locks could also be programmed to keep track of which card was used when; because staff members were each assigned a unique skeleton keycard, management could keep an accurate record of when workers entered or exited each room. The result was a drastic reduction in thieving employees.

Some hotels are now experimenting with even more high-tech locks, including ones that use iris scans, fingerprints, cell phones, and cards with radio frequencies that can unlock a door when swiped past a lock at close range. Hotels have been known to augur the future, offering us amenities long before we ever expected to have them in our own homes: gourmet food delivery, high-thread-count sheets, porn-on-demand. Most people still use house keys that are cut at hardware stores, but these might soon be going the way of museum collections, as well.

HOUSEWIVES

Married women who forewent having careers in order to take care of their husbands and children; similar to—but more demeaning than—the modern term "stay-at-home-mom." Tasks included laundry, grocery shopping, bed making, chauffeuring, and cooking, followed by Valium acquisition, bonbon consumption, martini preparation, and contemplation of the suppression of personal ambition. (NB: Though she wasn't really ill, she was sometimes aided by a little yellow pill.)

HYPHENATED LAST NAMES

Second-wave feminist trend of combining a husband's last name with a wife's to make one shared surname; spawned a generation of children who, upon marrying other hyphenates, had to drop one name, thereby showing the world which parent they loved more.

KEEPING PLANS (AND MAKING DATES)

The once-common habit of avoiding scheduling appointments, but honoring them once they were made.

• • •

Plans have become fluid—they have the ability to dissolve at any moment. Last-minute cancellations are now so commonplace that it's acceptable to make plans to discuss a plan—why decide now what you can decide later? "Sure," says the modern man. "Let's meet up on Tuesday, but let's talk that morning to figure out the details." Because if there's anything in this world that requires preemptive strategizing, it's lunch.

Particularly prone to this condition are plans that are made with those B-list people who hover somewhere in the gray area between pals and acquaintances. These are the people who might be your MySpace buddies, but will never earn myFaves status on your phone; the son of a family friend who contacted you for career advice; the sophomore year roommate who keeps throwing snowballs at you on Facebook.

Back in the day, many merely talked about making plans. The term "let's do lunch" was tossed around freely. Roughly translated, it meant, "One day in the distant future when I have my date book with me— one day in that happy time down the road when I will be out of debt and fulfilled and will have lost that last ten pounds and finally gotten through the pile of *New Yorker* magazines in my bathroom—we will again cross paths and at that point, we'll talk about making a plan to do something soon."

The popularity of Filofaxes in the 1980s and 90s created a slight increase in the likelihood that people would actually commit a date to paper, as it was important to make each page look as filled in as possible. PalmPilots had a similar effect—you didn't really want to have a catch-up drink with that coworker from three jobs ago, but if you whipped out your fancy little gadget it might get back to your old boss how well you're doing.

If any kind of date was actually made, it was usually for some far away Tuesday that seemed manageable if only because there were so many hours between now and then that "then" seemed like a reality that might never come to pass. In the event that the "then" date did actually roll around, the appointment was generally kept, barring some kind of emergency. Cancellations required calling and explaining why you needed to reschedule, and that meant hearing the person's disappointment or annoyance. And possibly faking a sniffle. In a pre–cell phone world, there was always the concern that you might not reach your date in person when you called to cancel. If you got the machine and were worried that she might not get the message before leaving the house, you had to wait to hear back in order to ensure that the message was received, or else you'd have to stomach the thought of her standing outside the movie theater in the rain for hours.

Modern technology, however, has made the impossible possible: We can go through all the niceties of making plans without any of the follow-through, allowing us to let people think we want to see them without actually having to inconvenience ourselves to that extent. If you're feeling lazy or if something better has come along, there's no need to do jumping jacks before dialing the cancelee's number in order to convince her how exhausted and overextended you are, or to force your daughter to cry in the background to back up your claim of being held hostage by an enraged toddler—a simple "I'm crazy busy today, can we reschedule?" via e-mail or text message does the job. There may still be some feelings of guilt involved, which is why we often wait until the last minute to cancel in the hopes that the other person might do the job first.

LANDFILLS

Areas created to store solid waste and mafia snitches, now highly regulated and even banned in some cities; a prettier word than "dump"; used to a great extent before all things became recyclable and peace reigned on Earth.

LANDLINES

Aural communication devices dating back to the late nineteenth century; considered largely indispensable, but often regarded with mixed feelings. As stated in the *Standard* in 1885: "There is some ground for hope the instrument may be improved out of existence shortly . . . and human life would once more return to those happier phases it knew before [Alexander Graham Bell] undertook to revolutionize it."

• • •

Not long ago, the idea of surviving without a home phone was unthinkable. We lived by the pulse of the rotary dial and the blinking, red hold button. We thrilled at all the opportunities and lives that existed between the covers of phonebooks (which, when retired, made decent booster seats). Even the cords, which eventually could be loosened enough so that they'd stretch through three rooms, were kind of sacrosanct: When they got knotted, we lovingly detangled them, or bought clever attachments to keep them from bunching up. Then there were all the lovely accoutrements: the silver phone dialers that acted as elegant finger-extenders, the telephone tables with a built-in seats you could wait at while you mentally coaxed the phone to ring, and Rolodexes (see page 148) that you'd casually leave flipped open to your most important contact. Getting rid of it all would be an abomination. Why not just go ahead and extinguish the sun?

Sure the apparatus had its flaws: Phone companies charged per minute, and the long distance costs could stack up quickly. Busy signals made you wonder if your grandmother was on the phone or if she'd collapsed and knocked the receiver off the hook; heavy breathers left you feeling violated. It also wasn't always possible to have a truly private conversation over the phone. In the days when operators connected

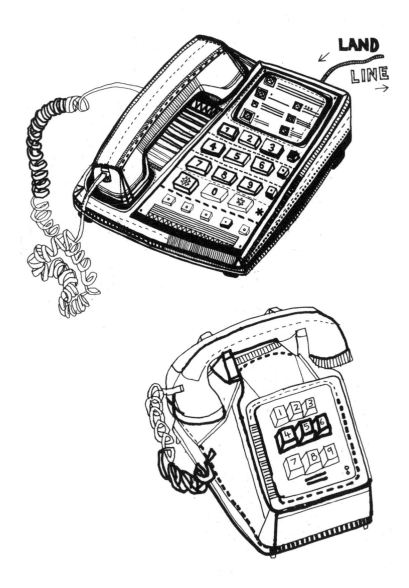

LAND
LINE

calls and separate families shared lines, you never knew who was going to listen in; he who planned a rendezvous behind his wife's back would have to develop a kind of code with his lover—one ring meant it was on, two would indicate a no-go. College students who wanted to escape the ears of a roommate either had to pull the receiver into the bathroom or else find a phone booth on another floor (although that meant gambling that it wouldn't be stuffed with half a dozen kids trying to set a record).

But there was still an undeniable magic to a device that made it possible to talk to someone wherever, whenever—and into a receiver that lived on Garfield's back, no less.

The telephone is a prime example of the way in which technology is reaching a kind of terminal velocity. Developments in communication didn't always happen at such a brisk pace. Centuries passed between the invention of moveable type in China and the printing of the *Gutenberg Bible* in 1454. It wasn't necessarily big news when it happened, if only because it'd be another four hundred years before the electric telegraph would make it possible to quickly convey news to other parts of the world. Even then, most people didn't have access to a telegraph and instead either traveled or used some kind of peripatetic intermediary in order to send messages across any distance. It wasn't until the 1870s that Elisha Gray and Alexander Graham Bell patented their early versions of the telephone. But by 1910, a quarter of households had them and, before long, it was possible to make calls from one side of the country to the other.

From there, the technology took off. Rotary dials began showing up in households in the 1920s, and operators started to become less essential (although dealing with them had never been such a hardship to begin with, considering they all spoke English). That was a transition that didn't sit well with people who'd grown fond of the women—they usually were women—in charge of connecting the lines. In the *New Yorker* in 1955, E. B. White complained that the telephone company needlessly "saddled us with dials and deprived us of our beloved operators, who used to know where everybody was and just what to do about everything."

Rotary phones gave way to touchtone ones in the 60s, delighting users who'd grown tired of waiting for the dial to return to its start position before keying in the next number. Then we were blessed with the conference-call function, call waiting, speakerphones, call forwarding, instant redial, and cordless receivers, which took some getting used to for people who were so accustomed to having all their conversations within viewing distance of the phone.

With each new advancement, the power structure between the caller and the callee shifted ever so slightly. For most of the phone's history, the caller was the boss, since he was the one to plan the call, and to pay for it. The recipient neither knew who was calling nor why nor when. Phone companies reinforced this power dynamic in their ads early in the century. "If any man in the Union rings the bell of his Bell Telephone at his desk, another man at the most distant point is in his instant command," read a 1909 magazine ad. "If I ring that bell, any man . . . is a prisoner." Indeed, there were many ways in which the receiving party was at the caller's mercy—she'd run to find the phone, possibly harboring a little fear about dealing with whatever unknown entity might be on the other end of the line. It could be, well, *anyone*. It was that feeling of vulnerability that birthed a hundred stories and films about mysterious callers who'd set off some kind of nefarious chain of events.

That all changed for good with the invention of caller ID and answering machines (see page 23). As we became less at the mercy of the caller, we also started to lose respect for the actual phone. For the bulk of its lifetime, the phone was a kind of member of the family; people even referred to the phone company as Ma Bell. But within the period of just a few years at the end of the twentieth century, it went from a respected elder that needed constant tending to something that could easily be ignored. We let cordless phones linger in between the sofa cushions, their batteries beeping for mercy. People screened their calls, or just categorically decided never to pick up the phone at all.

When we began making the shift to mobile phones, we started to shed so many of the ideas and habits we'd had about telephony for most of the twentieth century. No longer did we have to wait to use the phone until the household's teenager finished recounting every minute of her day (to a friend with whom she just spent the whole day), or rush around in a panic looking for change for a pay phone à la Dustin Hoffman in *The Graduate*. We even made peace with the fact that sometimes (and sometimes oftentimes) calls would get dropped. In the early 2000s, a growing number of families began canceling their home phones altogether. According to one survey conducted by an industry research group, in 2007, the number of cell phone–only homes surpassed the number of homes that had only a landline.

The advantages of using just a cell phone at home are hard to deny. You only need one, and you can carry it around in your pocket so you don't need to worry about having a different receiver in each room. Long-distance calls generally cost no more than local calls, and, because you're usually responsible for your own little device, there are fewer concerns about other people investigating your bill. Most of all, however, the shift has made call recipients feel less vulnerable: The caller has abdicated his position of power. Assured that you almost never have to respond to an unknown number or miss a call you're expecting, you've boldly decided to talk only when it was most convenient to you.

Indeed, talking on the phone at all is becoming increasingly rare, especially to a generation that, in 2007, crowned its first National Texting Champion: A thirteen-year-old won after typing a 151-character phrase in forty-two seconds. Many teens report that they can't recall when they last used their home landline, let alone memorized a number—an art which, much like dialing a number with fingers other than the thumb, is all but forgotten. It's estimated that close to 60 percent of eighteen- to twenty-four-year-olds in single-person households have no home phone at all. Kids younger than that often avoid talking on phones altogether, even when they have their own cells. According to Nielsen Ratings, kids thirteen to seventeen have an average of 1,742 text conversations per month, but make or receive only 231 calls. "My son refuses to use the phone—he texts, but he asks me to make calls for him and he never listens to his voicemail," says Bobbie, a Philadelphia mother of a sixteen-year-old. "It's like he just never learned how to have a phone conversation—how to deal with the pauses, or how to know whose turn it is to talk. It's almost as if he needs to come up with a whole planned-out script in order to not feel nervous about making a call." Once, when he told her that he was trying to make a call but no one was picking up, she took the phone from him and listened. "It was a busy signal," she says. "He thought that was just another kind of ring."

LATE FEES

Fines inflicted upon video renters who failed to return rented films by an agreed-upon date; acted as an incentive to both return rentals in a timely manner and to investigate other neighborhood video stores. Generally eradicated in the mid-aughts by the few remaining brick-and-mortar video rental stores (see page 179) after the proliferation of mail-order DVD rental services, which let users keep material for as long as they pleased. In 2005, the Blockbuster rental chain announced a "No More Late Fees" policy, but seemed to not quite get the idea. The company was sued by the state of New Jersey because, according to the Attorney General, they had "not told customers about the big fees they are charged if they [kept] videos or games for more than a week after they are due."

LAUGH TRACKS

Pre-recorded laughter injected into television sitcoms during the editing stage.

• • •

At the end of *Annie Hall*, Woody Allen's Alvy Singer is visiting an edit room where his friend Rob is tinkering with recently shot footage of his new show. Every few seconds, Rob instructs the editor to add a giggle or a guffaw after his TV self tells a joke.

"You better lie down. You've been in the sun too long."

Chuckle, chuckle!

"The limousine to the track break down?"

Ha, ha!

Alvy/Woody watches the whole thing with disgust.

"Do you realize how immoral this all is?" he asks.

Good news, Woody—you moral barometer, you: Today, laugh tracks are no longer a staple of sitcom edit rooms. The bad news? We might actually be laughing less as a result.

Laugh tracks were only a new take on an age-old custom. For centuries, theater owners filled audiences with people who were paid to laugh. In the 1800s in France, this practice birthed agencies, called claques, which represented professional laughers who would chuckle and titter at the appropriate moments. Professional laughers didn't make shows funnier, but laughter is scientifically proven to be as contagious as yawning, so a little laughter could quickly breed a lot. The more people laughed, the more likely the nonremunerated audience members were to enjoy the show. Or at least that was the line of thinking.

Because television sitcoms were often staged so that all the action took place in just a handful of static settings, much like a play, it made sense for early television producers to try to emulate theater. Adding laughter cues was a way both to encourage viewers to think a show was funny and to help at-home viewers foster the illusion of sitting in a live audience. When it became more common for shows to be shot in front of studio audiences, laughs were frequently still added to augment the studio viewers' organic reactions.

The Laff Box, a machine created in the 1950s, caught on quickly with editors because it let them add laughs using a piano keyboard–like system. Its creator is believed to have gotten the sounds he used for the device by recording people laughing during Marcel Marceau's famous mime shows. By and large, these are the same recordings that are still used in laugh tracks today.

"With laugh tracks, comedians were assured that if the audience members didn't laugh, they could make it sound like they did," says writer/director Larry Gelbart, a longtime critic of prerecorded laughter. "It lowered the bar for everybody. It lowered the bar for the writers who could be sure that what they were writing would be perceived as funny, and for the performers."

When he was directing the war-themed sitcom *M*A*S*H* in the 70s, Mr. Gelbart asked the show's network if they could be exempt from canned laughter requirements. He even conducted a test where two audiences watched the same episode, one with the laugh track and one without it. People in the laugh-track room probably did laugh out loud more than viewers in the other room, but when surveyed afterward, the groups reported enjoying the show equally. Still, the network bigwigs held their ground.

"They felt that the home audience would be encouraged to notice the comedy if 'others' were laughing," says Mr. Gelbart. "God knows where they thought the 'other' people were. Sitting in the foxholes?" He got the network to agree to let the operating room scenes be laugh-free. On the DVD release of the show, viewers can choose to turn off the fake audience. "If you listen to it with the laughs, it comes off as a smart-ass comedy which it wasn't supposed to be," he says. "They weren't supposed to be comedians or wise guys; they were just people observing horrible conditions and commenting on them."

Classic multicamera sitcoms where most of the action happens on just one or two sets—think *Friends* or *Seinfeld* or *Roseanne*—are being replaced by single-camera shows which are shot more like documentaries; there are more sets and fewer scenes that take place on a sofa. Instead of pausing for laughs from a real or recorded audience, actors work to illicit reactions from the people with whom they're performing, which lends these shows a feeling that's more natural than anything that, say, *Three's Company* was ever able to achieve. The further we go from sitcoms with theatrical-like staging, the less we are employing laugh tracks.

But the real cause of the demise of the laugh track may be the simple fact that we are no longer so accustomed to being entertained in groups.

"Before, there would only be one television set in a household. Now families are a lot more fragmented, and there just aren't the same opportunities to watch things together," says Mr. Gelbart. "People watch in their rooms alone, or on their phones, or online, or they watch while doing a million other things."

When alone, you're more likely to think "that's funny," although maybe without simultaneously blowing milk out of your nose.

At this point, the actual laughter we hear from Laff Boxes is coming out of the mouths of mime fans who are long dead. But the devices have yet to be completely discarded.

"One can only hope that one day they'll go away completely, but hope is a dangerous thing to have in television" says Mr. Gelbart. "For the moment, at least we can say that there certainly is laughter after death."

LAYAWAY

A store policy that allowed you to have a purchase held at a shop until you'd finished paying for it in monthly or weekly installments; often required dieting to ensure that purchased clothing would still fit by the time it made its way into your closet. Less evil than credit, but not nearly as fun.

LICKABLE STAMPS

Postage that needed to be moistened in order to adhere to an envelope.

• • •

In our germophobic society, it's easy to imagine that the introduction of a new piece of official currency that needed to be licked in order to be used would be met with more than a little concern. Yet for decades, you gamely opened your mouth and pressed a stamp to your tongue whenever there was a bill to mail or a letter to send. You didn't worry about where the thing had been, or who had touched it or whether it contained gluten.

Saliva-activated stamps are a reminder of a time when no one fretted over the possibility of getting poisonous powder or bombs in the mail; criminals didn't consider the ramifications of shipping a little sample of their DNA along with every ransom note they sealed in an envelope. Sure there were the occasional whispers of the cockroaches who lived off stamp-glue at Post Office storage facilities, but if you imagined them as charming little Jiminy Cricket–type creatures clutching their tummies in hunger, it was easier to shrug off that particular concern— and you could always get one of those spongy moisteners. The worst that could happen would perhaps be the occasional lingual paper cut.

First introduced in the 1800s, so-called "gum" stamps saved people the trouble of having to glue postage onto envelopes. For many a decade, they were considered a given. Indeed, gum stamps seemed like one of the more perfect inventions ever created: They were cheap, meaningful, attractive, functional, easy to use, portable, and even collectable. Few other essential desk-drawer objects did such a good job at activating so many senses: There was the raised feel of an engraved image, the eye-pleasing picture of a flag or Elvis or Tweety, the sound of the ripping perforations (fold, fold, tear!), and, of course, the unmistakable flavor of the cornstarch and dextrin that were combined to make the spittle-activated glue. In China, they took it one step further, making some of their Year of the Pig stamps taste like sweet-and-sour pork. Here in the US, the flavor was never anything special, but it was a constant that could transport you back to an evening of addressing wedding invitations, or that summer job where you discovered the meditative power of stuffing envelopes.

To the horror of the country's unruly philatelist population, the US Post Office began transitioning to self-adhesive stamps in the 1990s, partly in response to the complaints of soldiers in Desert Storm—the heat would cause their stamps to curl or stick together. There was also the *Seinfeld* phenomenon: When George's fiancée Susan died from licking envelopes, it was a bit of unexpected good press for the self-adhesive envelope industry. "When pressure-sensitive labels and envelopes started popping up, more people started saying to us, 'Why can't you do that with stamps?'" says David Failor, the Executive Director of Stamp Services for the US Postal Service. In 1995, only about 20 percent of the thirty-five billion stamps that the Post Office churns out every year were of the self-stick variety—producing sticky-backed ones was significantly more expensive than making the regular kind. But as they started to be printed in larger quantities, the machinery was refined, the supplies could be bought in larger quantities, and they soon were cheaper to make than the old lickable ones. They also were less affected by heat and better at sticking onto envelopes made of synthetic materials. What we've gained in convenience, however, we might have lost in other ways: Unlike gum stamps, pressure-sensitive stamps need to be sold in booklets, sheets, and rolls that have liners that can be difficult to recycle. In 2007, the California Integrated Waste Management Board even went so far as to issue a statement encouraging people to use moisture-activated postage as part of a waste reduction initiative.

Unfortunately, the old slobber-stamps are nevertheless getting harder to find at local post offices. "Most of the water-activated stamps we produce today are in large coils that go in older machinery that was designed to wet them and are still in use by some places," he says. Today, Mr. Failor estimates that less than 1 percent of stamps will ever make contact with a tongue.

LIGHTERS AT CONCERTS

The practice of bringing a portable lighter to a concert so that a small flame could be held overhead in order to indicate appreciation for a song. Most common in the period before Ticketmaster made concert tickets completely unaffordable; sometimes mimicked by a younger generation that uses cell phones instead of anything flammable. Fans of Bruce Springsteen, Bob Dylan, and the Grateful Dead all claim to have started the ritual, which some considered an attempt to recapture "the magic of ceremonial song—to evoke the flickering calm of the prerock era when music and magic had not diverged . . . This unconscious evocation of an ancestral, pre-elctronic past is entirely appropriate to the rock medium, since rock concerts have now taken the place of communal sacrifices, and performers have become our high priests."
—*Curious Customs*, 1987

LIGHTHOUSES

Structures that emitted beams of light to signal sea vessels. Once largely manned by monks who wouldn't have complained about living in a five-story walkup; first built by the ancient Greeks (who can take credit for the Pharos of Alexandria, one of the seven wonders of the ancient world). Also a staple of the collectible figurine market.

LONG-DISTANCE CHARGES

Per-minute fees incurred by landline phone calls that connected a caller to a party located outside the originating area code; still occasionally referenced when fishing for an excuse to get off the phone with grandparents.

MAIL

Pieces of paper used to communicate thoughts, feelings, and eviction notices, transported through a federally funded system that many people refused to call "socialist."

• • •

There's something magical about mail: Just a handful of change can ensure that a little piece of paper slipped into a blue box on the sidewalk will wend its way through some kind of Rube Goldberg–esque arrangement, transported to its destination by what must be millions of little green Doozers taping letters onto Frisbees. Or maybe by a fleet of surly Charles Bukowskis and Cliff Clavins pushing one-handled carts and driving trucks with right-hand-side steering wheels. Either way, the system seemed to work . . . most of the time.

For generations, mail was the cheapest form of travel. The simplest habits of letter writing—folding a sheet of paper in threes, writing out an address—were so commonplace that it's hard to remember ever being taught these skills. Today, these everyday motions are being performed less and less frequently. Thanks largely to e-mail and online bill pay, the number of pieces of first-class mail shipped each year has been steadily decreasing since 2005; between 2006 and 2007, the Post Office took a nosedive into the red when it witnessed its revenue decrease by close to 700 percent. The good news is that this means that this particular government agency is using fewer gallons of gas than previously and is creating less pollution. The bad news is that Doozers are signing up for unemployment—and communication may never be the same.

Sure, people always complained that it wasn't a reliable system. Things sometimes had a way of getting lost or arriving months after being sent. However, there was always some hope of one day recovering something that never got delivered—there was the possibility that there was some phone number somewhere that you could call that just might produce your missing QVC order. Today, e-mails that don't reach their recipients seem more likely to have vanished into the ether; good luck getting someone from Gmail on the phone to help you out with that. But misplaced written correspondence may still physically exist at one of the US's Mail Recovery Centers, where postal detectives try to determine the origins of the one million pieces of undeliverable mail that accumulate each year. Yes, much of it eventually gets shredded or auctioned off, but some of the more sentimental letters and objects are put aside for a time in the hopes that someone might claim them. If only your hard drive were so thoughtful.

The sturdy, dependable nature of a piece of mail is really the crux of its charm. Mail has long been a way of showing that you've taken the time to consider what you want to say to someone; phone calls and even e-mails don't require the same level of reflection. It's also a way of transporting a bit of someone's essence in a way that no technology since has been able to replicate. Even just a dashed-off note shows off your penmanship, your stamp choice; your return address label may belie your support of the ACLU. An envelope can even carry your scent—try doing that, Yahoo!. What's more, postcards and letters are objects that represent a specific moment and place in a way that an e-mail time stamp can't do. You might never make it outside of your hometown, but you can touch something that has traveled halfway around the world or that was postmarked more than over a hundred years ago. In second-hand stores and attic drawers, boxes of old postcards give us three-sentence glimpses into former existences, preserving candid snippets of lives long finished. E-mails printed out for posterity are likely to capture not nearly as many ephemeral details about your life other than, perhaps, the fact that your toner was low.

MANUAL CAR WINDOWS

Windows lowered and raised by non-electric crank systems in vehicles; required use of the elbow, shoulder, wrist, and fingers. Difficult to operate while also smoking, changing the radio station, talking on the phone, or making a left-hand turn.

• • •

The window crank was an object that imbued a car with a sense of fairness and symmetry: It gave the driver's under-utilized left hand something to do besides operate the turn signal, and one direction was no better than another, thanks to the fact that cranking clockwise would open the window if we were sitting on the right side of the car, or would close it if we were sitting on the left (this somehow made sense at the time, as if we were born with an innate understanding of vehicular ventilation systems). What's more, the window crank gave passengers some autonomy: Only the chauffeur could operate the gas or the breaks, but we could decide how the outside air would affect all the other riders' hairdos. These privileges were ripped away, however, with the introduction of the electric window, which gave the driver the power to determine every passenger's exposure to the outside world with just the push of a button. He could even lock the window altogether. Talk about indignities.

With a window crank, it was possible to open the window even when the battery was dead. Sometimes they'd stick or would need serious exertion to be opened, but you never had to worry that the dog might accidentally close the window on himself while sticking out his head. However, there was something less than suave about the manual window; It's hard to imagine a film where a villain or heartthrob slowly disappears behind a tinted window that, for a moment, reveals his elbow jerking in three-quarter time.

Electric windows were introduced in the US in the mid-twentieth century and were valued by manufacturers because, among other reasons, they could be placed in spots other than just under the window. They also streamlined the look of a car's interior, since cranks took up quite a bit of real estate on car doors. But up until rather recently, power windows were only standard in luxury vehicles. According to the auto data gathering company CNW Market Research, they were installed in fewer than 17 percent of cars in 1985; today, they're standard in more than 94 percent of new cars.

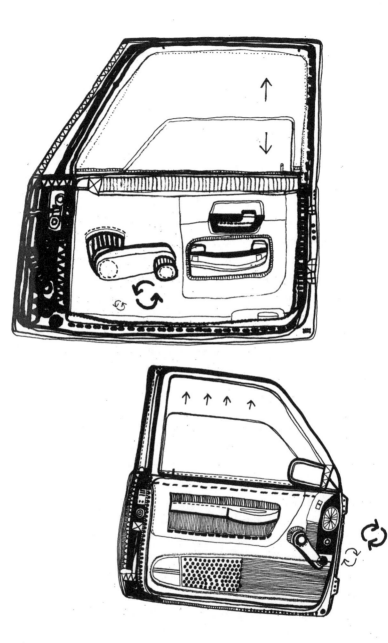

Power windows are one of many innovations that have supplanted old mechanisms in order to render today's average car more of a mobile living room than a tool we use to get from point A to point B. Only a small minority of new cars have manually adjustable rearview mirrors or non-power locks, for instance. Indeed, today many manufacturers bundle the workings of the automatic door locks, seat adjusters, speakers, and power windows into one complete module that can be easily shipped or replaced, an innovation that has streamlined the process and has made it, in many cases, cheaper and simpler to add these once "luxury" elements into standard vehicles.

The automation of our cars is making driving easier, but this is a mixed blessing. Push-button ignitions and doors that unlock simply by sensing the key fob in your pocket are the next steps toward helping even the simplest-minded, mechanically inept person get behind the wheel of a car.

MEETINGS

Face-to-face gatherings of two or more employees in office-based organizations; frequently conducted in order to discuss the proposed agendas of subsequent meetings.

MEN TREATING

Custom, employed during courtship, where the male party paid for dinner with the expectation that the female party would "put out"; collateral damage of the Women's Liberation movement largely replaced by practice of splitting the bill with the understanding that the man is willing to "put out."

MERCURY THERMOMETERS

Glass instrument containing toxic fluid; often forcibly put under a child's tongue. When intact, it could detect illness. When fractured, it could cause it.

· · ·

Encased in a thin tube with a vein of mercury ready to shoot up at the sign of a fever, the trusted glass thermometer was a scientific tool that served a useful purpose in the home, offering tangible evidence that you weren't well enough to go to school. Some went under the tongue, others were smeared with Vaseline and then inserted in the other end. Either way, there was often some confusion as to how long you needed to wait before taking it out—and then you had to figure out how to read the thing. By the time you located the tiny sliver of silver stuff, it was already starting to recede, which meant you had to shake it back down and start all over again.

Of course, if you weren't sure how sick you really were, a lightbulb held in close range of the thermometer's bulbous bottom could help you stack the case. Too close, however, and the little glass tool was liable to make you more than just fake sick: Excessive heat could cause the bulb to explode, and then you'd be covered with a substance that, even if only inhaled, had the power to make your kidneys and central nervous system go haywire. One gram of mercury, the amount in a household thermometer, is enough to poison the water in a twenty-acre lake.

Problem was, there were just so many ways to break them—and eventually, that's what seemed to happen at least once in every household. A small child forgot it was under his armpit. An older child, wise to the fact that a broken thermometer wouldn't stay below 98.6°, wondered if the thing would crack if he bit down. And wouldn't a mouthful of mercury mean that school was out of the question anyway? Even adults were known to drop them inadvertently. They were probably safest when used in the derrière, but . . . did you really want to go there?

Outside of their glass encasement, mercury droplets were neither liquid nor solid. They looked like hard little bits of silver, but then

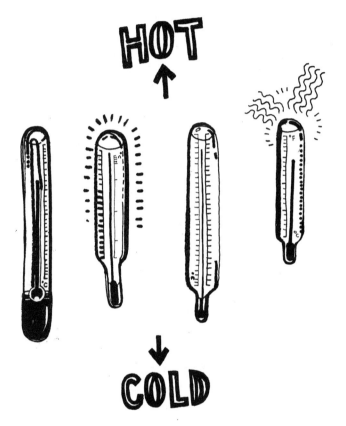

they'd slide around and mate with other drops, forming one big ball that could be slipped onto a piece of paper. It made for an awfully hypnotic toy. After the fun wore off, most people dropped the little globule into the trash.

It's been estimated that as much as seventeen tons of mercury is tossed every year. Much of it ends up in our water. And in our actors: When actor Jeremy Piven announced that he needed to leave his role in a Broadway production of *Speed the Plow* in 2008, he cited maladies brought about from mercury poisoning that he'd developed because of all the tuna in his diet. The press dubbed him the "human thermometer."

Accurate as that moniker might've been, it was slightly anachronistic. In 2001, the US Senate unanimously passed a national mercury thermometer sales ban. The next year, CVS, Rite Aid, and Wal-Mart started phasing them out completely, replacing them with glass thermometers that contain red alcohol, or digital versions, some of which can be used in the ear—and aren't ever fooled by lightbulbs.

MICROFILM/MICROFICHE

Spools of film or palm-sized transparencies that could hold an entire front page of a newspaper (both text and photos); often used to archive periodicals and viewed using a projector; used by sleepy teenagers in libraries in the 1970s and by the French military to transport and receive messages in the 1870s: They scaled down documents onto microfiche, then transmitted them via homing pigeons.

MILKMEN

Professionals who delivered dairy products, mostly milk, which came in reusable glass bottles that were not printed with information regarding pasteurization, presence of hormones, additives, calories, vitamin content, or missing children; usually were men accustomed to fielding winking comments about how much they resembled their clients' children; popular in the early and mid-1900s, but by 1975, fewer than one out of ten families had their milk delivered in this fashion. "When I was a milkman, I delivered mostly to households where the mother was home. But when both spouses started to work, people didn't get milk delivered so much," says Mike Smith, who was a milkman in Orange County six days a week from 1965 to 1980. "Everyone liked me back then. After that, I was a car salesman. No one liked me."

MINIDISCS

Short-lived kind of CD that allowed music listeners to erase tracks and make playlists, but had the misfortune of not being well distributed in the US until seconds before the iPod hit shelves; smaller in popularity than in size.

MISS (AND MRS.)

Honorifics that designate a woman's marital status; sometimes were used to passive aggressively comment on social standing or age.

• • •

When a stranger in front of you forgets to take her card out of the ATM or neglects to see the toilet paper stuck to her shoe, propriety used to call for you to yell out "Miss," or "Ma'am"—the closest female equivalents of "Sir." "Miss" was used for younger women. The first time you were labeled "Ma'am" was as memorable as the day you first noticed that your breasts were showing interest in meeting your bellybutton.

Today, however, in most parts of the country it isn't just women of a certain age who are falling victim to that nasal palindrome. When in doubt, people seem to feel that it's better to assume a woman is married and should be addressed as such, than to guess she is single. (Because everyone knows that married people are happier.)

In most parts of the country, "Miss" has fallen out of fashion when used with last names, as has "Mrs." Both are largely being replaced by "Ms."—a term that became popular in the twentieth century as a way to give women the option not to inform people of their marital status—an antecedent to Facebook's "It's complicated." It started out as an abbreviation of the term "Mistress," and can actually be seen on tombstones that are centuries old. It had slipped out of use until people in the mail-order business in the mid-1900s started using "Ms." on mailings because it was easier than trying to figure out which customers were married. In the 1970s Gloria Steinem, founder of *Ms.* magazine, urged that the term be readopted—men didn't need to announce their marital status every time they introduced themselves, so why did women?

The issue came to a head when Geraldine Ferraro ran for vice president in 1984. She requested to be called "Ms.," as opposed to "Mrs." The latter, she felt, would be misleading, because Ferraro was her maiden name, not her husband's name. On the other hand, "Miss" would've erroneously suggested she wasn't married. It was at that point that "Ms." started to seem more like a practical solution than a statement about gender and equality, and "Miss" and "Mrs." began to feel a little stuffy and antiquated.

But today, all these terms are teetering on the brink of irrelevancy, thanks to the fact that we've become cavalier about using first names.

"People no longer address letters, for example, with honorifics. They just put bald names down," says Judith Martin, the syndicated etiquette columnist known as Miss Manners (although some newspapers have indeed replaced even her column's "Miss" with "Ms."). Mrs. Martin (as she likes to be called) argues that people's confusion about which appellation to use for women has ultimately caused us all to become less polite. "'Ms.' is an extremely useful designation, but there's been a tremendous resistance to it, and that's led to a rather promiscuous system where there is no standardization of names or titles, which leads people to get fed up with trying to figure out which one each person likes. Instead, they use first names in circumstances which are not connected with any sort of intimacy or friendship, or even acquaintanceship. It used to be that when someone said, 'Oh, please call me by my first name,' it was kind of an honor and a sign of warm friendship. Nowadays, someone could call you and might start using your first name. They even will make a nickname out of it, and it could be a salesperson making a cold call."

Familiarity, in other words, is no longer viewed as something that may be inappropriate in some cases. Says Mrs. Martin: "It's as if we're all instantly friends."

MIXTAPES

Audio cassettes recorded with songs that were carefully collected from records, the radio, CDs, or other audio cassettes; often created and then gifted during courtship.

• • •

Mixtapes were the pre-MP3 playlist option for the young music lover who wanted to play tracks by more than one artist without sinking coins into a jukebox or hopping off the couch during a make-out session. Painstakingly recorded from the radio or copied from other people's music libraries and then labeled with loopy script or scribbled drawings, these aural diaries defined our breakups, our summers, our crushes. They gave every fourteen-year-old the ability to play both DJ and album cover artist without leaving his bedroom. All it took was two little buttons, some time, and a lot of heart.

The mixtape was a kind of currency that has yet to be replicated—a tangible way to quantify your love of music or your love for your lover. Is the recording missing the first few bars of "Total Eclipse of the

Heart"? That would just show your ersatz Molly Ringwald that you cared enough to spend the weekend running to the tape deck every time a song you were waiting for came on the radio. Or perhaps you were industrious enough to call the radio station to make a request, catching a little bit of Malibu Sue's intro just in order to make sure you didn't miss any part of the *bum-ba-da-bum-ba-da-bum-bums* in David Bowie's "Under Pressure."

A good mixtape was a badge of honor. Your friends at summer camp all clamored to copy the rap compilation mix you made—but was it DJ Jazzy Jeff that they loved, or was it you? In the era of the homemade cassette, these sorts of distinctions were hard to make.

In 2007, Jason Bitner, cocreator of the magazine *Found*, came across a mixtape that his middle-school girlfriend had made for him in the 1980s. The discovery led him to post recordings of other people's mixtapes on his site CassetteFromMyEx.com. "There are parts of the tape I found where I could hear the warbling of a record or I could hear her put the needle down on the record," he says. "The process informed the concept. You'd have to listen to each song as you made it while recording it. When I listen to it now, I realize that I'm not just hearing the songs, I'm really hearing the process she went through to record them."

But the mixtape, like the audio cassette itself, has become a relic of ancient times, replaced instead by CD compilations and traded playlists—neither of which involve the same level of effort (or, ahem, artistic aplomb) that the making of a mixtape required. These formats allow the listener to easily shuffle tunes, ignoring the fact that the precise ordering of the tracks was arguably the most important part of sharing music. The songs built to a crescendo, or alternated between male artists and female ones, or started off with proclamations of love spoken through Stevie Wonder's dulcet tones, then suddenly switched to the "Folsom Prison Blues" (hey, you don't want to seem *too* into her). For the mixtape devotee, the track order of certain tapes is so burned into the memory that, even out of context, it's impossible to hear the end of one favorite song without immediately recalling what the next one should be.

Those dying to cram in as many songs as possible (filling up that last minute with one of the standard quicky songs: the Violent Femme's "Old Mother Reagan," Simon and Garfunkel's "Bookends," The Beatles' "Her Majesty". . .) would sometimes use a 120-minute tape instead of the typical, sixty-minute one; it was a move that only betrayed a kind of greenness, since any savvy mixtape-maker knew that the ribbon in longer cassettes was thin and ergo prone to breakage. Sometimes the tape would flip over and the opposite side would play backward, forcing you to have to unscrew the whole cassette to fix it. Or it'd get caught in the tape player in the car and then would get all crinkled. But then you'd hear that part when you were listening to it some other time and even the mangled bits would become part of the experience, because you'd remember where you'd been and what you were going through when it originally got damaged.

Niggling matters such as illegal duplication and copyright infringement never entered the mind of the mixtape maestro. Those were simpler times—and there were more subtle laws to abide. (As the music-snob protagonist mused in Nick Hornby's novel *High Fidelity*: "You can't have white music and black music together, unless the white music sounds like black music, and you can't have two tracks by the same artist side by side, unless you've done the whole thing in pairs . . .")

Subsequent music-recording technologies lack the same ephemeral quality of the homemade cassette—unless many copies were made, a broken or lost mixtape was not an easy thing to replace. They were objects imbued with drama: They could be stamped on or torn apart or thrown in a fit of breakup rage, but they could also be lovingly taped back together, or rewound with a pencil. When it comes to matters of the heart, iPods are better at keeping their distance.

MSG

Seasoning blamed for headaches, often consumed in food that left you feeling hungry even before the delivery guy had gotten back on his bike. Short for "monosodium glutamate." Also short for "made stuff good."

NEWSPAPERS

The daily happenings printed on inexpensive paper; often black-and-white, formerly read all over.

• • •

In the book *The Vanishing Newspaper* (unfortunately, a work of nonfiction), journalism professor Philip Meyer crunches the numbers: By his calculations, the last newspaper will go to print in 2043. In the fall, to be precise.

This is a calculation that would seem off the mark to anyone who has taken public transportation in the twenty-first century: It's been quite a while since the bulk of the passengers at rush hour could be seen folding their papers into expertly constructed quarters, or else stretching broadsheets halfway into their seatmates' laps. Crossword junkies are more likely to be found staring at their iPhones. On the streets, honor boxes often aren't refilled for days on end. Even dog owners have made the switch to plastic bags.

In the aughts, newspapers around the country found themselves in the painful position of reporting on the shuttering of the print editions of one competitor after the next, many of them casualties of advertisers who'd been wooed away by the charms of pay-per-click banners and Craigslist. 2007, 2008, and 2009 were particularly bad years: Rest in peace, *Baltimore Examiner, Cincinnati Post, Albuquerque Tribune,* and *Kentucky Post* and *Madison's Capital Times,* and *South Idaho Press* and *New York Sun,* and the list continues, but this is turning into a run-on sentence. Print-lovers wrote editorials that pooh-poohed the practice of skimming down a screen; publishers pointed to studies that show

diminished levels of comprehension when reading news online.

There was plenty of reminiscing about mornings spent breathing in the smell of newsprint while assessing a black-and-white facsimile of all that had happened and would happen and might happen. People blamed the economy. People waxed nostalgic about inky fingertips and walking outside in stocking feet to rescue a paper lodged in a hedge. People lambasted Bush the Younger for undervaluing the importance of the Fourth Estate. People went online and came up with suggestions on how to save the industry (Subsidies and endowments? Print on electronically charged plastic? Edible paper!). People did a lot of things . . . except buy more newspapers.

Why plunk down a quarter (or two or eight) when there's so much good news offered for free on the Internet? Heck, you could just go online and write your own darn news. Journalists were used to getting paid next to nothing, but it turned out there were quite a few writers in the world for whom no pay was just enough.

We like to think that newspapers are as old as time, but the kind that we are most familiar with has been around for less than two centuries; it's only a couple decades older than the fax machine (see page 73). Newsboys first hit the New York pavement selling penny papers in the 1830s, each edition filled with local stories and sensational foreign news. Prior to that point, American newspapers had been slim, pricey, business-focused communications only intended for an older, elite stratum of intellectuals, many of whom worried that cheap papers heralded the death of journalism. Of course, affordable paper didn't bring about the end of the printed page. Today, however, the popularity of free online news means that daily newspapers are read by a scant 19 percent of American adults under age thirty-four, and an older, elite stratum of intellectuals worries that this is the end of the road for the inexpensive periodicals they cherished. The average person picking up a hardcopy at a newsstand is fifty-five.

This revolution—or evolution or devolution, depending on whom you ask—has been a while in the making. The most recent proclamations that the end was near were in the 1960s; newsroom editors were rankled by Marshall McLuhan's descriptions of a culture that was weaning itself from newsprint in favor of more "horizonless, boundless" types of media. A lot of fingers pointed to TV news as the culprit. "Television threatens to engulf the written word like a blob from outer space," wrote one *Newsweek* columnist in 1968. When the *San Francisco Examiner* began providing the paper digitally in 1981 to people who had home computers, the local KRON-TV newscaster did a news story on it, suggesting that their efforts were inevitable but unripe. The clip showed an older man dialing a number, then resting the receiver on a device that was hooked up to his computer; two hours (and $10) later, he was able to view the paper's text on the screen. The newsman explained: "This is only the first step in newspapers by computer. Engineers predict that the day will come when we'll get all our newspapers and magazines by home computer, but that's a few years off." Then the camera shifts to a portly newspaper salesman, and the newscaster's voice raises slightly in pitch, suggesting he's about tie up his story with a cute kicker (something potentially dripping with sarcasm and hyperbole): "So for the moment at least, this man *isn't* out of a job."

Even then, however, newspaper readership was on the decline. In 1972, 70 percent of people read the paper every day; by the late 1980s, that number was hovering at approximately 50 percent. By 2000, it was 35 percent. The irony is that a decline in newspaper readership doesn't mean that people are reading less news. In fact, they're likely to be reading more: According to a Gallup Poll, the number of Americans getting their news online in 2008 was more than four times the number of people who were reading print versions of national newspapers in 2004. Very little of that information, however, is stamped with the authority of a newspaper byline, or written by the quintessential cynical-but-objective reporter—the kind who has as much ideology in his whole body as the average person has in his pinkie.

Internet news, with all its "citizen journalists," may not always be reliable, but that might not be such a problem for many readers. Surveys have long suggested that a sizable chunk of the newspaper-buying population lacks total confidence in the veracity of all the printed content they consume. (It didn't help the matter when, in the 90s and aughts, a string of journalists at reputable publications were caught making up stories.) What the Internet may lack in terms of accountability, it makes up for in breadth and customization, allowing users to create a kind of personalized aggregation culled from independent blogs and online versions of respected sources. There will just be a decrease in the chance that any of the stories in that digest will also be printed somewhere on a piece of paper that'll hit your doorstep. Still, one way or another, the information is being shared. And it won't ever turn yellow.

It might be redundant to continue feeding mammoth rolls of newsprint into printers located on the outskirts of cities around the country, but that hasn't kept the industry's giants from trying to keep their heads above water. The dissenters, however, are watching the clocks. When the *New York* Times trimmed the width of its paper in an attempt to cut costs in 2007, there were smirks among those who prefer reading their news on screens. "One and a half inches down," wrote one commenter on the *Times*' site. "Twelve inches to go."

NICHE PUBLICATIONS

Magazines that catered to readers with specific interests, ultimately viewed as too pricey to print. 2009 saw the demise of:
Book World
Cigar Report
Country Home
Domino
Furniture Style
JPG
Mountain Time

Private Air
Simple Scrapbooks
Traffic World

. . . along with more than thirty-five other publications. And that was just in the month of January.

NUNS

Female Catholics who took vows of chastity and wore black-and-white habits—either because it was a way to escape the path of marrying and raising children, or because they truly wanted to devote their lives to Jesus; some worked at schools attended by Martin Scorsese. In the 1960s and 70s, many women left con-vents—some because they saw that there were more options open-ing up for women who did not want to marry, and others because they disagreed with the Pope's stance on the Vietnam War, abor-tion, and birth control. In 1965, the US was home to 179,954 nuns; by 2006, there were 67,773; their average age was sixty-nine.

PAPER PLANE TICKETS

Vouchers for travel by way of airplane, mailed to the purchaser and frequently lost somewhere between home and airport.

PASSBOOKS

Stapled booklets that were stamped at each visit to the bank in order to record deposits, withdrawals, and interest; superseded by mailed bank statements and super-superseded by online banking. Employed by the unfortunate souls of the pre–ATM era who could only access money if a bank was open.

PAY PHONES

Public coin-operated telephones, often with cords wrapped in metal in order to deter vandals. To the chagrin of many a drug dealer, AT&T disconnected all of theirs in 2008. Some were located inside of booths that were used as time-travel apparatuses by Bill and Ted in their "excellent adventure" and as a changing room for Clark Kent (who eventually was forced to make do with a revolving door). By most calculations, New York City has only four booths remaining, and the DC area, a mere one.

PENNIES

Coins representing one hundredth of an American dollar, once used for purchasing candy, now used decoratively in jars. (*Also see Cash*)

PERCOLATORS

Coffeemakers that pushed boiling water up through a cylinder into a chamber of coffee grounds, producing a brew that smelled better than it tasted and was imbibed from cups that were referred to using the English words "small" and "large."

PERSONALS

Short postings in the back of newspapers purchased per line alongside the apartment, used-car, and escort listings in the "Classifieds" section; usually took the form of an advertisement, extolling the writer's virtues and then describing his or her ideal mate. Frequent abbreviations included:
> DWM: Divorced White Male
> LTR: Long-Term Relationship
> SBF: Single Black Female

VGL: Very Good Looking
NLP: No Losers Please
GSOH: Good Sense of Humor
BHM: Big Handsome Man
OHAC: Own House and Car

PHONE SEX

Arousing conversations conducted via telephony, sometimes for a fee; born in 1875, with Alexander Graham Bell's first words into a phone: "Mr. Watson, come here. I want you."

• • •

"My work was communicating with people using technology that only utilized our voices. My role was part sexual entertainer and part therapist," says Vixen, a longtime phone sex operator based in Santa Fe. "I was the perfect friend or girlfriend—always happy to hear from you and always eager to talk about what's on your mind." Alas, there are fewer places that are still offering this kind of customer service. Dial-a-Porn services, those 900 numbers followed by seven, artfully strung together letters (HOTGIRL, SEXBABE, etc.) that first cropped up in the 1980s, have seen a decline in business in the last five years—why pay per minute for what you can get free online?

When the phone sex industry was in its prime, many knew the mix of excitement and frustration experienced while waiting for the operator to connect a customer to a phone sex operator (anticipatory minutes well captured in the inimitable Village People music video for their song "Sex Over the Phone," circa 1985). The phone sex devotee knew how to cradle the phone just so in order to have two free hands, and usually had enough imagination to banish any concerns that the person on the other end of the phone might not actually be everything she said she was. He also was adept at doing the song-and-dance routine that'd be required in order to convince a spouse that those charges that had ended up on the bill must be a mistake. (If the phone company could be persuaded to remove the charges, they'd generally block all subsequent calls to pay-per-minute numbers.)

But the real blow is more likely being felt by those who liked dabbling in phone sex with non-strangers, mostly because there are now just so many advantages to being an SMS or AIM Casanova: You need not worry about phone bills or eavesdropping roommates; images can be swapped quickly or even live; and most IM nookie and text sex can be pursued right at the dinner table or office desk, under the guise of getting homework assignments or checking the human rights situation in China. It's also low effort (the IM orgasm requires little more than holding down a couple of vowel keys and hitting return, then gracefully exiting the situation with a quick BRB or TTYL), and can be saved for later enjoyment (command-C, command-V, and voilà). It's safer than actual intimate congress, and has less of an ick factor—no fluids are exchanged, no sheets need be cleaned, and, unless it's a good wireless hotspot, airport bathroom stalls can be avoided completely.

With virtual reality programs like Second Life, people create avatars of themselves and go on to have illicit affairs and even long-term relationships, often conducted solely with staccato onscreen messages. Then there are services like HighJoy.com, which send users Internet-enabled sex toys that can be plugged into one's computer and then manipulated by a partner at a separate computer using controls located within an instant-messenger box.

For many, inhibitions and embarrassment seem to be smaller issues onscreen than on the phone, especially with strangers. But a certain level of intimacy is lost. A lover who isn't well-read might sound like Lauren Bacall on Skype, but come across with all the passion of Ikea's Anna operator bot over Gchat. A certain cadence can easily be lost; giggles are gone; pauses all the more fraught (is he reaching for lube . . . or concurrently IMing another girl?). There are also the problems of losing humor and irony in a format where tone is hard to convey, as well as the grand potential for misunderstandings. "Oh, God!" could become quite an awkward phrase if your typing paramour happens to be dyslexic.

While it's doubtful these media could ever threaten the popularity of the actual act, there's no shortage of people eager to experiment with them. According to a survey conducted in Canada for the site CampusKiss.com, more college students take part in instant-messenger sex than in any kind of telephonic sex.

Because love means never having to say, "Can you hear me now?"

PHOTO ALBUMS

Bound books, often sizable and fitted with plastic sleeves or notched corners, used for displaying printed photos that were kept for posterity if only because it wasn't possible to delete them.

PHOTOBOOTHS

Coin-operated machines that produced strips of damp, odiferous photographs several minutes after pushing a button; publicly located devices that allowed lovers a few minutes of privacy inside a small, dark chamber.

PLASTER CASTS

Powdered gypsum used to stabilize broken bones; replaced by lighter and faster-drying fiberglass wrappings that do not provide smooth slates for the scribblings of middle-schoolers.

PLASTIC BAGS

Carrying devices once given away for free at supermarkets to people who eventually grew accustomed to getting the evil eye from those who brought their own hemp totes; always needed to be doubled up (it was always unclear why manufacturers didn't make half the quantity at twice the quality); banned by some municipalities in the late aughts, including San Francisco and Los Angeles (which estimated that city residents had been using five billion of them each year).

POCKET PROTECTORS

Synthetic sleeves kept in shirt pockets in order to keep pens from leaking on clothing; invented in 1952 by a PVC manufacturer who absentmindedly put a checkbook cover in his pocket when taking a phone call. They became irrelevant once BlackBerries were kept in pockets instead of Bics; an internationally recognized symbol of nerdiness.

POLAROIDS

Instant memories, squared.

• • •

Lynnette Astaire, a New York City artist in her twenties, is in love with her digital camera. "I call it my husband," she says. That doesn't mean, however, that there isn't place in her heart for previous lovers. Her first romance holds on to an especially large chunk of her soul: He was a red-and-black Polaroid 600 whom she first met when she was seven. That's why, when she learned in February of 2008 that the Polaroid company would stop producing film before the year was out, Ms. Astaire went into an extended period of mourning. She donned a black veil and organized a funeral procession, complete with pallbearers, a New Orleans jazz band, and a custom-made casket big enough to fit several of the now-vintage cameras.

Ms. Astaire was not alone in her strong feelings. The company's grim announcement resulted in damp tissues all around the world. Photographers loaded up on thousands of dollars worth of their Polaroid film of choice, while amateurs dug out their dusty devices and debated

whether it'd be wiser to use their last shots in memoriam or to hoard their film indefinitely. Art schools around the country changed their syllabi. A flurry of e-mail petitions zoomed around the Internet, while people swapped ideas about how the old Polaroid factories—located in Massachusetts, Holland, and Mexico—could be bought and salvaged. A couple of well-intentioned websites popped up to offer online ways to manipulate digital images so that they'd get the blurry and tawny look that people associate with Polaroid photos, but they offered little solace. A few days after the news broke, London Fashion Week's daily paper printed an obituary for the film. Naturally, Ms. Astaire could relate. "For me," she says, "it was like my first boyfriend had died."

The death was far from instant. There had been attempts to revive their brand for years. Efforts included ill-fated mini-Polaroid stickers and matte prints that you could write on, but the company still suffered for more than a decade. Fact was, the sixty-year-old Polaroid just wasn't as instant as it used to be. The minute it took for the image to develop used to seem incredibly fast compared to the hours or even days it would take to get standard film developed in a lab. By the early 2000s, however, digital photography made a minute seem like sixty seconds too long. No, you can't hold and save a digital image stored on your hard drive, but the majority of amateur photographers preferred the ease with which digital photos could be stored and shared online. By 2008, it was easier to find a store selling a picture of the adored camera printed on a hipster T-shirt than it was to find the actual film; having been defeated by digitization, Polaroid had officially joined the ranks of Che.

The first "instant" camera, the Polaroid Model 95, was a folding contraption invented by Edwin Land and released in 1948. The idea for a camera that could instantly produce prints dawned on him when his young daughter asked him why she couldn't see photographs immediately after they were taken. The smaller Model 20 Swinger became available in 1965. Like its predecessor, the picture could only be seen once the negative was pulled off the back of the print, but it was simplified so that any amateur could use it, and it was affordable, to boot. This incarnation of the device, and the little wallet-sized black-and-white photos it produced, was such a success that the entire first batch was bought up within one week.

The company didn't really hit its stride, however, until 1972 when it introduced the SX-70 Polaroid folding camera. These beautiful cameras, with their leather shells, rubber bellows, and shiny-smooth buttons, were small enough to fit in a suit jacket pocket. You pushed the button and then—*click, zzzzp, ka-dunk*—out burped a little dark square that would transform into a fridge-door-ready version of the sun teetering on the edge of the horizon, or the perfect cake you'd just made. And it only took a minute. The prints had that iconic white border, the bottom of which was three-quarters of an inch—just big enough that you could write the date on it with a Sharpie or hold it without smudging the photograph.

There were no wires to connect. No drugstore was needed to process the film. There were also no guarantees. If you smiled funny in this picture, if someone's elbow inadvertently slipped into that frame, you weren't just going to toss it. On a digital camera, you might press delete; with regular film you can just choose not to make a print from a particular negative. But because Polaroids developed on the spot, they didn't afford the photographer those kinds of luxuries. Instead, you slipped the undesired photos into a shoebox, not realizing that one day, those little imperfections in the shots might just make them all the more appealing. You had dozens of photos of Aunt Martha flashing her big gums, but with hindsight, you would probably be glad that you had captured her grimace, too. There were also little flaws that took you by surprise: occasional errant blobs of developer burned the film, an overexposure created images that were half-brown. The images weren't always perfect facsimiles of the world around you, but they were pictures with soul, nonetheless.

We've long been taught to distrust things that are packed with chemicals or that offer gratification that seems too instantaneous, but the Polaroid spat in the face of all these assumptions. Ansel Adams loved them, as did the DMV and modeling agencies, and the elf who took pictures of kids sitting with department store Santas. They were the cameras of choice in doctors' offices, and were beloved by impatient children, but they were also utilized in the studios of fine artists who found ways to manipulate the chemicals to create color bursts and distorted images. Passport issuers had them, and professional photographers came to rely on them in order to test their lighting before they committed to using regular film for a shot. Andy Warhol famously used his to take quick pix of all the men who came to his parties, but only after he'd convinced them to remove their pants. Indeed, the Polaroid was the ideal technology for capturing those private moments that weren't meant to be seen by anyone who worked at Walgreens.

More than anything, it was an equal-opportunity art form. "If you took a brilliant Polaroid, it wasn't because you had a great camera, or because you had an amazing subject, or vast knowledge about the medium. It was because everything happened to come together just so. In that way, it evened the playing field," says Amit Gupta, founder of the photography website and newsletter Photojojo. "The closest thing that we have to that right now is all the artists and regular people alike who are going around taking pictures with their iPhones. They're crap cameras, but that makes it all the more interesting when you're able to use them to make something really beautiful."

PORNOGRAPHIC MAGAZINES

Glossy periodicals containing nude photos, but really only purchased for the articles.

• • •

Internet porn: It has helped colloquialize terms like "money shot" and fanned the careers of such notable characters as Lexington Steele and the inimitable Buttman.

It's also taken away Al Goldstein's reason for living.

"I was a pioneer," says Mr. Goldstein one autumn evening in 2008. "But now, there's no room for me."

Mr. Goldstein, now in his seventies, is best known for creating *Screw* magazine, an unapologetically lascivious tabloid magazine that prided itself on its high level of raunch and complete lack of taste. He also was the host of *Midnight Blue*, a long-running adult-themed public-access show which no one liked and everyone watched.

But both achievements were only relevant in the days before the Internet, when the only way to instantly obtain a free photo of a naked woman was to find a Polaroid camera (see page 134) and a girl interested in seeing your etchings.

In Mr. Goldstein's formative years, photos weren't even part of the equation. "I was in a boys' school and the only thing I could get my hands on were novels by Frank Harris or Henry Miller—five or six pages would get me hard, but it was all from their words into my imagination, no pictures," he says.

For men who came of age before the web, scoring pornography called for forethought, money, and sometimes ID. It demanded a level of exertion—it at least required standing up (even if you had a magazine subscription, the mailbox wasn't going to walk to you). Kids rifled through parents' and older siblings' nightstands in the hopes of finding a crisp *Penthouse*, only to end up settling for the sex scenes in a dog-eared edition of Judy Blume's *Forever*. For those who actually made it all the way to the store, a porn purchase demanded the ability to fish out the desired item from behind a wall of dusty Plexiglas—and to stomach the embarrassment elicited by seeing the flash on the face of the checkout boy when he realized *Bear* was not a periodical about stuffed animals.

Pornographic magazines still exist, but their relevancy has taken a nosedive. It's also become hard to define which magazines are "porn" and which are mainstream, thanks to the fact that even women's magazines today often feature thong-wearing wraiths on their covers.

The first technology to take a chunk out of the porn magazine business was the videotape, which made it possible to watch pornographic movies in the privacy of one's own home. The Internet, which has been a major porn portal since the 1990s, took an even bigger bite out of both the magazine and the video markets. The first images sent online—Internet porn's Lascaux caves, as it were—were of naked women rendered using a kind of dot matrix made out of rows of punctuation. How far we've come . . . Today, if you can dream it, you can find naked pictures of it online. There's even an open-source site, PornForTheBlind.com, that invites people to narrate the action in porn films for the benefit of the visually impaired:

> *A blond gentleman is getting out of his truck. It's a bright, sunny day. A woman with large bosoms is in a blue dress. It is a surprise birthday party for this gentleman and now he's in a room with four women. One of the women grabs his penis and sticks it between her bosoms; that doesn't look right. Damn, she's got a nice ass, you've got to see this! Oh, that's right, you can't see . . . well, picture a watermelon, but really soft . . .*

Penthouse, which in the 70s sold upward of five million copies a month, wasn't selling half that many a year by 2008. *Hustler* saw its circulation go from three million in the 80s to roughly seven hundred thousand in the last twenty years, says its founder, Larry Flynt. "Why pay $7 when you can get it free online?" says Mr. Flynt when reached in his office. "There'll always be people who want to feel a magazine in their hands, but the Internet is an option for people who just want porn and don't care much about editorial content or entertainment value."

Magazines, of course, had their benefits. They were more mobile than laptops; you didn't need to find a good wireless signal to use them; they fit so nicely under a mattress. If you had one delivered, there was the joy of anticipation for the next issue and the mixture of excitement and concern that a neighbor might see it on your doorstep. Some of them had an added bonus: great cartoons and articles. Really.

In the height of adult magazines' popularity, they also were a medium that provided an odd sense of camaraderie that has arguably been lost. In the days when there were only a handful of pornographic glossies to choose from, that month's centerfold could be certain that at any given moment there were trillions of little sperm landing in tissues because of her and her alone. (If this thought never crossed the model's mind, her father probably thought it for her.)

Whether the Internet is the reason that we're living in such a porn-obsessed time or merely a product of our compulsion, it's impossible to deny the desensitizing affect it has had on our perceptions of sex. Even sheltered children and teens today can't avoid being exposed to banner ads that lure visitors with bulging cleavage and spam offers assuring that you'll be able to add five inches to your johnson with just a double-click. Pornography has melded seamlessly into our everyday lives; it now exists on the same screens on which you edit Word documents and pay bills. Sasha Grey and photos of your friends' new babies can exist in abutting windows on your desktop.

The decline of the magazine has only heralded the rise of pornography's acceptance. In her book *Pornified*, author Pamela Paul talks about how we've become so nonchalant about porn that TV shows like the stripper docudrama *G-String Divas*, or *Private Stars* (where men and porn stars are locked in a house together), or *Can You Be a Porn Star?* hardly register on our cultural radar. Paul notes that when *Playboy* turned fifty in 2003, its editor-in-chief, Hugh Hefner "was treated like an elder media statesman," with a profile in the *New York Times*. Christie's auctioned off mementos of his career. "Pornography has not only gone mainstream," she writes, "it's barely edgy."

Is the change of our preference for pornographic intake a sign that we are becoming more open-minded or more depraved? Al Goldstein believes it's only a sideways step. "Porn is stunted. It's a retarded child. There's no where for it to go. Men are still walking dicks, and whether they're looking for women online or at a bar or in a magazine, it's the same thing. Does it matter what the format is?" he asks, wheezing into the phone. "I don't think it does. But I was unequipped to step into this technological world. I've fulfilled my purpose. Now I think I'm going to go kill myself."

PRIVACY

Keeping your business to yourself.

• • •

In his 1964 book *The Privacy Invaders*, Myron Brenton wrote that society was on "the threshold of what might be called the Age of the Goldfish Bowl . . . A couple of generations hence, will some automated society look upon privacy with the same air of amused nostalgia we now reserve for, say, elaborate eighteenth-century drawing room manners?"

You bet.

Secrets were once precious nuggets that existed only in whispers and in the pages of the locked Lisa Frank diary you kept under your mattress. You didn't have to worry that anyone would look in your bag at the airport—why would little-old-you garner that much attention? Not everyone had to know via eVite that you were attending Helen's Surprise Party ("With bells + 1"); there was no instant public announcement that you'd transmuted from "married" to "single." And, when you spoke of celebrities—where they shopped, what they did with gerbils, whose cousin's step-brother's uncle had slept with Tom Cruise—it all fell under the umbrella of gossip and rumor. There was an unspoken understanding that even public people were allowed to requisition some degree of privacy. So what if there wasn't a way to verify who was pregnant or whether or not a celebrity frequented Wal-Mart, "just like US!"; postulation offered a lot more opportunity for the imagination than fact.

The demise of privacy can be hard to separate from a rise in immodesty, but the latter will never supplant its prudish relative. Modesty goes in and out of style. In the twenty-first century, we're as accustomed to nudity in art as the ancient Greeks and Romans were, but that doesn't mean that the intervening millennia didn't see years of brandished fig leaves and hidden ankles. One era's taboo subject is another's dinnertime conversation.

But the existence of the Internet makes it hard to imagine that privacy will ever return to its pedestal. Once, if you were a young starlet, you might be okay letting magazine subscribers pay for the privilege of seeing you nude. Or not. Today, a modest woman isn't given a choice: Just because she hasn't welcomed that kind of exposure doesn't mean when she's exiting a car, there won't be photographers zooming in in the hopes that she forgot to wear panties.

Part of our obsession with eradicating privacy may stem from an unparalleled desire to stand out from the crowd and not be forgotten. For ages, an amount of anonymity in life was a given. Milkmaids and blacksmiths begat milkmaids and blacksmiths, and their lives generally went undocumented. Perhaps we are now simply cashing in on all of those unused fifteen minutes of fame. Watch one episode of *American Idol*'s audition week and it's clear that people will gladly mortgage their privacy if it means a chance at celebrity; fame has become an almost universal ambition, although you might be willing to settle for the constant recognition and attention that can come from regularly updating your MySpace page or using a blog to discuss the length of your fingernails—posted with the assumption that people care.

An unfaithful spouse, a negligent parent, a flasher—all can and do have their identities exposed, so to speak, on the Internet, and usually with little consequence to the secret's unveiler. The Patriot Act and other amped-up security measures that have come into existence in the last decade have further enforced the idea that private information can be a dangerous thing. Then there's the fact that an explosion in media of all kinds has created a constant need for content and characters, and a neverending surplus of people scrambling for the limelight.

Others opt for validation by exposing everything from heartbreak to heart surgery to the speed of their sperm on reality television. Either way, being seen by an invisible public is the goal. In a 2006 poll of British ten-year-olds, "being a celebrity" was voted the #1 "very best thing in the world." God was tenth.

There was a major whiff of privacy's swift-approaching devolution when the documentary *An American Family* aired in the 1970s featuring edited footage from three hundred hours that a film crew shot of a real

Santa Barbara family in their home. Brows furrowed over the appropriateness of showing people suffering through major family crises for the purpose of entertainment, even if they'd agreed to the experiment. By the 90s, however, unveiling people's private lives became the stuff of big business. Celebrity magazines went to new levels to chronicle the minutiae of stars' lives—even the president's genitals were no longer off limits as a topic. The question of ethics was pushed aside, as was the idea that people needed to be privy to the fact that their lows were fodder for popular entertainment. Couldn't we just assume everyone wanted that kind of exposure? America mocked this shift in perception with *The Truman Show*, a movie about a man who was unaware that his life was the subject of a TV show. But just a few years later, so many mentally unstable people had delusions of grandeur that involved being followed around by cameras that the epidemic was labeled the Truman Show Syndrome.

In the late 90s in Japan, the assumption that people would be lucky to have their private lives publicized was taken one step further when a weekly "reality" television show called *Denpa Shonen* featured a naked man locked in a room where he had to subsist on only what he could win from sweepstakes advertised in a pile of magazines he was given. His placement in the room was the prize he received after winning a raffle; he wasn't told he would be filmed. He went long stretches of time crying and eating nothing but rice cooked in a tin can. The crew left him in there for more than a year before they told him that his confinement was being broadcast all over the country.

The show received stellar ratings.

PUSH-BUTTONS

Three-dimensional circles or squares that turned on the coffee maker, started the dryer, and provided a subject for elevator conversation.

• • •

One morning in the mid-aughts, more than a thousand employees of the News Corporation offices on Sixth Avenue in Manhattan stumbled into the high rise's elevators, Venti coffees in hand, only to find that something had changed their commute forever: The elevators' buttons had disappeared.

News Corporation's "destination lifts" are among several thousand elevators around the world operating without buttons in the cars. Some require that the passenger press a button for their floor on a panel outside the elevator bank; a screen then flashes a letter that indicates which elevator they should take in order to get to their desired floor. With other models, passengers need only use a key fob in the elevator bank to tell the elevator to take them to the correct floor. Schindler, the Swiss company that makes these elevators, hopes eventually to produce models that can operate purely by voice recognition.

Destination lifts are just one of the recent blows to push-buttons. On the one hand, we are more dependent than ever on buttons—we're constantly using keyboards on computers and phones and PDAs. But we're also phasing them out, thanks to devices like touch-screen tablet PCs, iPhones, Mac laptops that have no mouse buttons, voice-recognition software, and laser devices which can project a usable keyboard onto any flat surface.

The springy turn-things-off-and-on kind of button we're accustomed to today was born about a century ago. According to product designer and button historian Bill DeRouchey, the first ones could be found on portable flashlights that came on the market in the 1890s. In the early 1900s, Kodak popularized the devices, which were sometimes called "electric snaps," on cameras. Prior to that, camera shutters had to be opened and closed manually in order to expose the film. When they introduced the Brownie, Kodak's first push-button camera, the company created a slogan that captured the essence of the new technological era: "You push the button, we'll do the rest."

By the century's end, button pushing had become both a skill and a danger: What if the president confused his nuclear bomb detonator

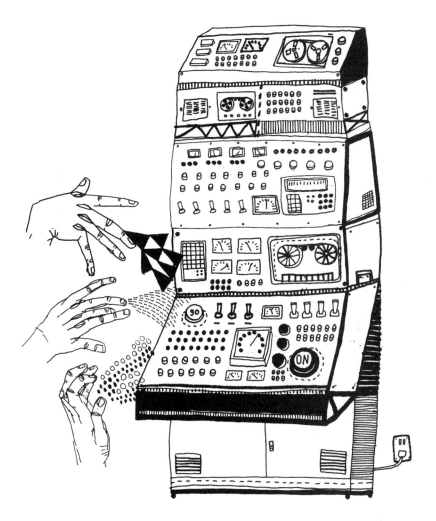

with his Donkey Kong controls?

Good old spring-loaded push-buttons, with their clickity sound and satisfying cause-and-effect nature, are still as easy to push as they ever were, but in an effort to simplify and streamline every aspect of our lives, we've decided that our fingers are too precious to do so much work. With the introduction of Apple computers, buttons migrated onto screens, where they live as symbols. At first, there were actual button-like icons on computer screens indicating where we needed to click in order to make something happen; now, buttons have largely lost their physical shape on screens and instead are found in the form of icons. We usually still have to push down on a mouse's button in order to interact with links, but it's such a wimpy kind of pushing action that it's almost insulting to compare mouse buttons to, say, the little red guys on the old Nintendo consoles. Now *those* were buttons.

Of course, the slow move to abolish the button is part of an effort to make complicated devices seem simpler and more user-friendly. Buttons used to be objects that symbolized intelligence—in cartoons and movies, complicated panels of buttons always signified something brilliant or sinister. More modern devices like the iPhone, the iPod, and the Wii are so streamlined that they're almost button-free. "You don't need to exert yourself," they seem to say to us, winking with a single Cyclops-like button. "Just push me in this one spot and I'll figure out the rest." In other words, our devices have learned to push their own buttons.

Some manufacturers prefer virtual buttons to physical ones because a device's software and programming can be changed much more easily than its outer casing. Apple can add usability to the iPod or iPhone ad infinitum without ever changing the physical casing of the product, which of course means that they need to figure out other ways to get you to replace your brand new iPod with a brand-newer one.

Part of the eradication of buttons relates to the movement to make life as hands-free as possible. Why flush a toilet when it can be programmed to do it for you? Why dirty your hands on the faucet when it will shut off automatically? In the end, however, making things less manual is making us less connected with objects than ever. Devices seem more like foreign things that are only minimally within our control—and that may only be making things more complicated.

This was apparent one afternoon when Mackenzie, a News Corporation staffer, watched a visitor try to navigate the building's elevators. "Karl Rove came into the building and I watched him get into an elevator, but he didn't know the system," she says. "I could see his mind working, looking for buttons, but there were none. I just grinned at him as the doors closed, ready to take him to some mysterious random floor."

ROLODEXES

Spinning desktop aggregators of contact information that could second as flipbooks or low-fi air conditioning.

• • •

Brooklyn-born inventor Arnold Neustadter didn't like disorder. "If I took a phone message for him, he wanted to know everything—first name, last name, where they were calling from, why, their number, the time . . . and I was just a little kid!" says his sixty-year-old daughter Jane Revasch. "He was extremely precise."

His address book, however, presented a kind of mess that he couldn't quite harness. Mid-century families were infamously peripatetic. Vaguely dissatisfied despite being well-clothed and fed, and in possession of a nice station wagon and a decent wet bar, they determined that the real American dream existed just two suburbs over: Between 1948 and 1970, an estimated 20 percent of all Americans moved each year. How was anyone supposed to keep track of all those new street names without having to rewrite their whole address book every few months? This dilemma was coupled with fact that, as the first decades following the invention of telephony started piling up, an increasing number of businesses had phone lines; address books had to store an entirely new category of information on top of everything else. Phone numbers changed even more often than addresses: If someone was promoted, he might have a

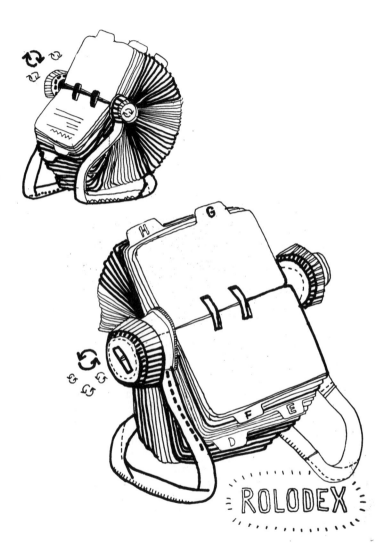

ROLODEX

new office in the same old building, but he'd get a new phone number, resulting in more pages cracking with Wite-out, entire sections extracted, blacked-out entries, and new zip codes scribbled in margins (there was a moment in 1967 when all zips were converted from two digits to five digits, resulting in *lots* of changes). When there was no longer room under M, a coda symbol would have to indicate that those entries were now being placed in W. The S's were mostly residing on an inserted piece of paper clipped to the back cover, and any completely new entries were just going to have to wait until you could find a replacement book. Further complicating the issue was that sometimes all this painstakingly copied contact information belonged to people who had the nerve to die.

Mr. Neustadter had combated office disorder before. His weapon of choice? The "dex." His Swivodex was designed to prevent ink bottles from spilling; his Clipodex was a device that attached to the knees and helped stenographers keep their pads from moving; the Punchodex was a kind of hole-punch. In the late 1940s, he and a designer came up with a possible way of dealing with the address book dilemma: propped-up rotating wheels fitted with inexpensive removable cards; some models had locking covers (most people were not aware that every lock took the exact same key).

All in all, it was an elegant solution. The cards were removable so that Q didn't have to take up any space at all if it had no entries—the circular design allowed the more demanding letters of the alphabet to have more space when needed. If a company moved, their card could just be tossed and replaced.

Yet people were slow to catch on to the device that he'd named the Rolodex. When Mr. Neustadter first started selling it in the 1950s, stationery shops were skeptical that anyone would want the spindly device on their desk. By the 80s, however, the Rolodex had become such an icon that lawsuits were filed by companies who accused former employees of taking them with them when they left—having a Rolodex filled with important names meant everything. There were models selling for more than $200, and people often valued them at prices far higher than that. An entire 1986 episode of the TV show *Moonlighting* was devoted to one stolen Rolodex being held ransom for $50,000.

But could you really put a monetary value on something that could organize everything from account numbers to birthdays to the prices of pepperoni pies at the best local pizza places? While the manufacturers gave no suggestion for the best use for a Rolodex, they were mostly used to organize phone numbers and addresses and were kept on desks— the perfect mascot for workplaces that were putting an ever increasing value on connectedness. In 2008, Stanford University professors found that the average Facebook member aspires to have around three hundred friends, but that would've seemed a piddling number to the average Rolodex devotee, who often made it a point to use as many cards as the contraption could allow—and some held up to six thousand.

At his long pinewood desk, Farrar, Straus & Giroux president Jonathan Galassi has five well-worn Rolodexes that he's collected over the last thirty or forty years, each one jammed with cards—some typed, others written out in his meticulous longhand. "These cards hold my history," he says, thumbing the cards, many of which have phone numbers that are likely obsolete. One gives the phone number of photographer Annie Leibovitz, back when she was still with the late Susan Sontag; another is for a pre-fatwa Salman Rushdie. Sometimes he goes through and pulls out cards for people who are dead or who've faded from his memory, but there are some defunct entries that he leaves in for sentimental reasons. "Here, she was my teacher at Harvard," he says, plucking out a card for former poet laureate Elizabeth Bishop, who died in 1979. "This was her address on Brattle Street in Cambridge, but then she moved. Here was her number when she was in Maine one summer. There's a whole history of my relationship with her, all on this one card." These days, he often uses an address book on his PC, but he still lets his Rolodexes occupy a certain amount of precious desk real estate. "I guess one day I'll have to throw them out . . . " he says wistfully.

Some people were first lured away from Rolodexes years ago when the Filofax started gaining popularity. Paul Smith, the men's clothing designer, kicked off the trend when he started selling them at his stores in the 80s—they hinted at a business-obsessed culture that was growing outside of the realms of the office. They married the address book with the date book, and took a cue from the Rolodex by using binder clips and fungible pages. What's more, they were portable. But they were less perfect substitutes than the PalmPilots, BlackBerries, Outlook address books, and iPhones that supplanted them.

Mr. Neustadter, who died in 1996, never saw the way in which digital storage would affect his iconic invention. But his daughter insists he would've argued that his brainchild was as relevant as ever. "Computers get viruses," she says, "But the Rolodex—it's never taken a sick day in its life!"

That said, she admits that she doesn't use one: "I've just never been that organized."

SADNESS

A sorrowful emotion that did not require a doctor's attention.

• • •

When Bobby McFerrin sang "Don't Worry, Be Happy," in 1988, Americans took it as an order. Once upon a time, people were either bummed-out or joyful, moody or stable, crazy or sane. Today, if you're not on some part of the depression spectrum, then you're likely a touch bipolar, or ADHD, or obsessive-compulsive—all terms that would've elicited an awkward silence if spoken at the dinner table two decades ago. Now, a conversation devoid of the term might sound a little bit like silence.

As antidepressants have become more refined, marketed, safe, and available, crying into your pillow while blaring Leonard Cohen and reading *Anna Karenina* has become a kind of crime. When *Death of a Salesman* was revived on Broadway in 1999, the *New York Times* declared: "Get that man some Prozac!"

"Kids today are growing up with drugs being advertised on TV like

toothpaste, and consequently are being instilled with the idea that you can rid yourself of untoward emotions. They're made to believe that you can go from crying and holding your head to running in the sunlight," says Charles Barber, author of the book *Comfortably Numb: How Psychiatry Is Medicating a Nation*. Mr. Barber points out that in 2005, more money was spent in the US on the antidepressant drug Zoloft than on Tide laundry detergent, and in 2006, nearly ten times as much was spent on antipsychotics than in 1996. These pills might result in lower sex drives, but who cares? We get to be happy! Oh, joy! Sit down, rapture! Have a Corona! War? Bore! Worried about laugh lines? We can cure those, too (See *Wrinkles*, page 182).

It's hard to say whether or not we're really better off living in a world where boilerplate sadness is often diagnosed as biological depression, and depression is considered anathema. What's clear is that we have a better understanding of the chemical causes of certain conditions and a greater sense of why our brains work the way they do. While this is a good thing for those of us wondering why a happy childhood still resulted in years of mild malaise and head shrinkage, it's great news for anyone whose life has been completely paralyzed by depression and uncontrollable emotions.

For what it's worth, sadness had an awfully good run before its current exile. "In the 1800s, Thomas Carlyle talked about how happiness was really only a few hundred years old," says Mr. Barber. "Before that, people were too busy trying to survive and fight off Cossacks to even think about emotions, let alone the idea of being 'happy.'"

SCRIPT

(*See Cursive Writing*)

SECRETARIES

The office gatekeeper whose role was similar to that of the modern administrative assistant. "You hear the word 'secretary' and the image that flashes through your mind is a girl in an office who types for her living. That's not far wrong. In the United States, there are about 2.5 million such girls—or ladies, to be more polite and to take proper account of the fact that nearly half of them are married women. Your only mistake—and to call it a mistake is almost a quibble—is that you've forgotten that men (even boys) can also be secretaries . . . [They] should not be confused with 'typist,' 'junior stenographer,' or 'stenographer,' for, properly speaking, a 'secretary' is more than any of these." —*The Wonderful Writing Machine*, 1954.

SHORT BASKETBALL SHORTS

Thigh-exposing bottoms worn by NBA players.

• • •

The practice of playing games in retro uniforms is common in basketball now; it gives teams another jersey to sell at the concession stands. But in late 2007, in a game against the Boston Celtics, the Los Angeles Lakers took it one step further—they wore throwback shorts. As in short shorts. For anyone who has mourned the days when a player's full legs were as conspicuous as his tattoos, it was a moment of glory.

A brief one. The Lakers immediately fell behind. Despite a halftime change to the usual baggy, floor-scraping kind of shorts. Perhaps the players being shell-shocked from the sight of their own upper thighs caused them to lose the game . . .

"I don't know what it feels like to wear a thong," said Kobe Bryant after the game, "but I imagine it feels something like what we had on in the first half. I felt violated. I felt naked."

How times have changed. Short shorts now look as anachronistic on the court as the thirty-second shot clock or the red-white-and-blue balls that were mandatory on the American Basketball Association's

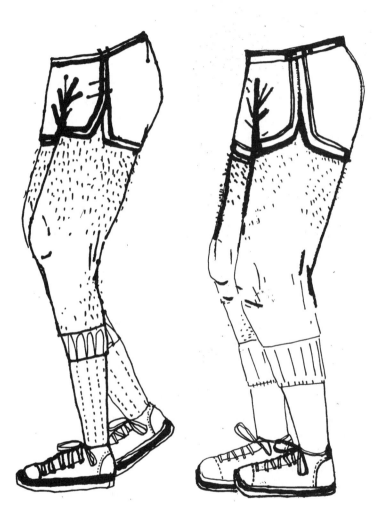

courts (until the National Basketball Association absorbed that league in 1976).

Not long after ABA fans adjusted their eyes to a new ball color, they had to reformulate their idea of proper play attire. In 1983, Michael Jordan showed up at North Carolina with an extra couple of inches on his shorts, reportedly because he liked having extra fabric to dry his hands on when they got sweaty. The look quickly was adopted by men and boys nationwide, and hems as well as waistbands have only continued to travel southward. The last holdout was Utah Jazz point guard John Stockton, who remained loyal to the short shorts look, but when he retired in 2003, so did the era of visible knees.

SHORTHAND

Any of a number of stenography systems taught before the prevalence of tape recorders and word-processing software that involved using abstract symbols and abbreviations in order to write quickly; often used when taking dictation or recording notes on an event. Notable texts originally written in shorthand: *The Diary of Samuel Pepys* (1660–1669), a document considered one of the most important of its era; Woodrow Wilson's "Fourteen Points" speech, leading to peace following World War I (1918); and the minutes of the biannual shareholders meeting of the Combinex Mutual Insurance company of Kansas City (1972), a turning point in the question of whether the second parking lot gate should be kept locked after 7:00 P.M.

SINGLES BARS

Dimly lit establishments where unmarried people could gather in person (i.e., without the shield of a computer monitor); served many a young professional hoping to meet a desperately lonely alcoholic to bring home to mom.

SKATE KEYS

Tool for tightening the leather straps that attached platform roller skates to sneakers, often worn on a string around the skater's neck; a device which many considered to be vaguely sexual after the release of Melanie's 1971 hit single that contained the lyrics, "Well, I got a brand-new pair of roller skates/ You got a brand-new key/ I think we should get together and try them out, you see." This was despite Melanie's insistance that there was no sexual innuendo in the lyrics. Her next hit song was about how much she disliked her previous single.

SLIDE PROJECTORS

Devices which made it possible to blow up transparencies and display them one at a time to deeply interested dinner-party guests.

SMOKING

Odiferous (but enjoyable) way of committing suicide on the installment plan.

• • •

At 3:30 P.M. on April 1, 2003—a day as good for midday drinking as any other on the calendar—there were only five people in the normally packed Nancy Whiskey Pub on New York City's Lispenard Street.

But outside, the bar's regulars swarmed, cigarettes and cigars in hand. New York City's ban on smoking in bars and restaurants had been put into effect only days before.

One smoker, Jimbo Hodgdon, a jovial, tattooed ex-trucker, biker, and machine-shop manager of North Bergen, New Jersey, had been a Nancy Whiskey regular since 1975. He described the scene.

"When I arrived, there were ten people outside," he said. "There were more people outside than inside, and the people inside were complaining that they had to go outside to smoke. And then the bartender,

she comes out and says, 'Somebody was smoking in the ladies' room! Do you know they're bringing in sniffers?' And I said, 'Sniffers? Listen, I'm the best panty-sniffer in town!' And she said, 'No! Sniffers for smoke in the bathroom!'"

Toodleoo, smoking.

In the months and years that followed, dozens of other states and cities, including Boston, DC, and Chicago, all instituted similar bans. Much of the world likely chalked it up to more puritanical Americanism—another quirk of a country with fluorinated water and wars packaged with catchy slogans. How, they asked, could you possibly score a date at a bar? But in January of 2008, the City of Light itself started popping Nicorette. Paris, once a place where a diet of espresso and Gitanes was *comme il faut*, has now banned smoking in all restaurants, bars, and theaters.

The cigarette's history is so intertwined with sex and reckless youth that it's hard to imagine a world that's completely "no smoking." Would John Wayne have been the same kind of iconic presence if he had been chomping on carrots? And yet, so many tobacco-related cultural markers have become distant memories: the post-coital drag, the kindergarteners charged with making ashtrays out of clay, the smoke break (a good enough reason to take up the habit to begin with). There was also all the lovely paraphernalia: monogrammed cigarette cases and Holly Golightly–esque holders, purse-sized silent butlers, and big Ronson table lighters that looked like little art pieces.

But it's hard to argue with jurisdictions that will likely drastically decrease the country's cases of emphysema and lung cancer (as well as leukemia, cataracts, pneumonia, premature births, abdominal aortic aneurysms—I'd go on but I've only been allotted a couple hundred pages for this book). What's more, we are tasting our food better than ever, and can now awaken after a night of barhopping without smelling like the love child of Bette Davis and Popeye.

Spain, France, Australia, South Africa, and the US are among the countries that saw cigarette consumption decrease by at least 10 percent between 1998 and 2008, according to the World Health Organization. The American Lung Association estimates that in the US, we smoke two thirds the cigarettes today that we did in 1990, thanks both to greater awareness about the harms of smoking and to price increases that have made cigarettes practically luxury items in the States. If cigarette dispensers still dotted the earth as they once did—those well-lighted machines that provided tobacco to anyone of any age with just the satisfying pull of a knob—they'd require at least two bulky-pockets worth of quarters to get just one pack.

"I can hardly afford it anymore," says Mr. Hodgdon, still a Nancy Whiskey regular. "They put a little porch outside of Nancy's with French doors, so we go out there to smoke. But still I don't do it so much anymore. When I'm there, I don't smoke as much, or else I just don't go there. I like to go to a bar, sit down, have a little libation, and smoke. If I can't do that, then what's the point?"

Unfortunately, the fact that there may be fewer smokers here doesn't mean that their global population is dwindling. Westerners may be slapping on nicotine patches, but the number of smokers in poorer places in the world continues to grow. The American Cancer Society estimates that 84 percent of smokers live in developing countries. There are currently 1.3 billion smokers worldwide; according to the ACS, that number will hit two billion by 2030.

It's almost enough to drive you to drink.

SOCIAL E-MAILING

Form of communication employed by adults to keep in touch and make plans, often used when they have their Outlook open at work anyway; this type of social interaction is increasingly spurned by people born after 1990, who prefer forms of electronic communication that are more immediate, less likely to pile up, and more spam-resistant. (This means a future decrease in interns with e-mail variations of xoxKateLuvsRainbowsxox@gmail.com.) According to a 2006 survey conducted by the consumer research company Parks Associates, teenagers are less likely to use e-mail than any other demographic: Fewer than 20 percent of thirteen- to seventeen-year-olds use e-mail to communicate with friends.

Emily Siegel, seventeen: "I use it for, like, reaching my coaches or uncles—old people. Otherwise, it's either my cell phone or Facebook."

Logan Rothman, sixteen: "I check it maybe once a week. I've never used it to keep in touch with friends. I can imagine using it for work one day, but I'm not sure why I'd use e-mail for anything else."

STOVETOP POPCORN MAKERS

Metal pots fitted with cranks for churning corn kernels. Produced a salty, buttery snack that took approximately 8 percent as much time to consume as it did to prepare. In the mid-1900s, lost some of its market share to less labor-intensive stand-alone electric popcorn makers and to Jiffy Pop, which made it possible to heat up corn kernels in a one-time-use pan. The Jiffy Pop foil pan was covered with a paper-and-foil balloon that would expand with heat and would catch the popped corn. All three methods were largely eradicated by microwavable popcorn, which was faster to make than it was to eat, thereby totally missing the point.

SUPER 8s

A type of film cartridge developed by Kodak in 1965 that contained 8mm film which, unlike previous models, was preloaded into a cassette; could record up to four minutes of grainy footage at a time (sound recording capabilities were added in the 1970s); abdicated its throne upon the arrival of the never-to-be-improved-upon VHS tape.

TELEX MACHINES

Telegraph printing-cum-typing machines first developed in Europe in the 1930s, used for the purpose of transmitting information as noisily as possible.

THESAURUSES

Numerically coded reference books that contained synonyms for the purpose of making a person sound smart, adept, clever, nimble, astute, shrewd, or wise.

TOKENS

Currency that was used to get on the subway, play video games, redeem free drinks, and—in the case of college brochure photos— display the acceptance of minorities.

TONSILLECTOMIES

An operation that resulted in a strict diet of ice cream.

• • •

For the bulk of the twentieth century, tonsils were practically considered optional, and more than a few kids rubbed their throats and made puppy-dog eyes at their parents in a calculated maneuver that would likely get them a few days off from school—not to mention the special treatment, popsicles, and copious gifts that were crucial to the recovery process. An overnight stay at a hospital was a must, but tonsillectomies were considered such minor surgeries that children, carted off to the stuffed-animal-laden children's wings of hospitals, often treated the stays as mini-vacations in exotic new places full of exciting, foreign objects: stethoscopes, paper nightgowns, IVs. For most kids, it was a rose-colored first view of a place that didn't yet equal illness and death. Sure, there was the rotten-carrot smell of the mask that the anesthesiologist used, and at least a week of throat pain, but these were small prices to pay when you took into account all the sherbet and Jell-O and pudding that suddenly had your name on it.

For decades the procedure was seen as a requisite rite of passage in a kid's life; the majority of patients were under fifteen. Remiss was the family who ignored the possibility—nay, *probability*—that their tykes would need the procedure; concern over a child's tonsils was as much a sign of considerate parenting as clean fingernails and piano lessons.

Perhaps that's why in the mid-twentieth century, tonsillectomies accounted for roughly one out of two operations performed in the US. Chronic sore throat? Upper-respiratory infections? Tonsillitis? Little white tonsil stones sticking to them? Out they came.

"It is not definitely known how many persons possess infected tonsils, but to unprejudiced observers they appear to be as universal in all civilized countries as is the use of handkerchiefs," Pulitzer Prize-winning historian Kenneth Roberts wrote in 1936, soon after he got his own pair extracted (his doctors promised, somewhat inexplicably, that removing them would alleviate a pain in his knee). "In spite of the prevalence of infected tonsils, nobody ever has a good word to say for them. In fact, nobody has even been heard to speak kindly of tonsils that are healthy—perhaps because there are no healthy ones."

Doctors often removed the adenoids along with them—a snoring solution for the pre–Breathe Right nose-strip generation. But it was an operation that wasn't without serious risks. In the 1950s, it was estimated that in the US as many as one in five thousand tonsillectomies resulted in fatality.

Tonsils started to get pardoned when a 1963 British study found that there was little difference in the long-term health of children who got their tonsils out and those who kept them. Largely as a result of that study, the number of tonsillectomies performed each year has steadily dropped. By 1990, it was performed on fewer than one hundred twenty thousand American children under age eighteen, according to the Center for Disease Control; by 2000, that number had dropped to just over twenty thousand.

But our hesitance to mar the throats of young people via surgery doesn't reflect any kind of increased wariness about the risk factor of other surgeries. You might be met with shock if you ask a doctor to take out your tonsils in order to give you some respite from seemingly chronic sore throats today, but mention that you've been considering a surgery for cosmetic reasons and you're unlikely to find a surgeon who'll discourage you. We willingly volunteer ourselves for optional surgeries performed for reasons slightly less dire than tonsillitis: Wrinkles are now reason enough to befriend a scalpel, as is an aquiline nose. Even birth can usually be scheduled and performed in the OR if that's what a patient wants.

However, there is good news to be had: An increase in the performance of optional surgeries like, say, liposuction, only means that the few who still get seemingly necessary tonsillectomies can eat their Häagen-Dazs with all the more impunity.

TRADITIONAL NAMES

Popular monikers given to many children of each generation; designations prided for their normalcy as opposed to their creativity; for extreme cases, see offspring of: Foreman, George; McCave, Mrs.

• • •

On a summer day in 2008, Pamela Redmond Satran was at a farmers' market when a man ran by chasing after his toddler. "He was yelling, 'Odinn! Odinn!'" recalls Ms. Satran. "I suddenly thought, 'Oh my god, what have I done?'"

Ms. Satran, the coauthor of the baby naming book *Beyond Jennifer and Jason*, has long been a believer in the importance of giving children unique names, but in recent years, she's started to wonder if things have gotten out of hand. "When all the toddlers in the playgroup are named Jupiter or Antigone, it makes me think that maybe we've gone too far," she says. "Recently, I was sitting next to parents who had a little baby named Barbara, and I thought, 'Wow! How counterintuitive!'"

The popularity of popular names is on a swift decline. It's becoming less common for teachers to have to use the initial of a kid's last name in order to distinguish her from all the other Jessicas in the room, and more common for them to ask parents for pronunciation pointers.

For most of American history, there were only a handful of names that appeared on any class list. In 1900, more than 15 percent of boys were named John, William, or James. "People wanted to be like everyone else. Immigration was an influence—people wanted to blend into society and leave their ethnic names behind," says Ms. Satran. But by 1997, only 5 percent of baby boys received the top three names (Michael, Matthew, and Jacob), and by 2007, that number had been nearly halved. The most popular name for girls today is Emily, but when Jennifer first became the number one name for girls in 1970, it was found on the birth certificates of twice as many girls as Emily is today.

Picking a one-of-a-kind name for a child is a matter of utmost importance to the modern parent. You might not be able to predetermine your baby's hair color or taste in music, but you can give him a moniker that will ensure that he'll be unique—or laughed at. Either way, choosing a name has become a power trip enjoyed by many a mom- and dad-to-be. Forget Tom, Dick, and Harry—think Inspektor Pilot, Hopper, and Audio Science (the actual names of the sons of, respectively, actors Jason Lee, Sean Penn, and Shannyn Sossamon).

"I think it has to do with the rise of brand awareness—we've come to recognize the meaning of, say, big interlocking Cs on a handbag," Ms. Satran says. "I think our obsession with brands has had a subliminal influence on people thinking about their child's name as something that's an important part of how they'll be seen by the world."

Search engines have also affected parents' thinking. Pick a name with enough vowels and apostrophes and you can be fairly certain that no one else will pop up when future employers Google him. This seems important, until you realize that it means your thirteen-year-old's Jonas Brothers tribute page will also likely be easily findable in Google's cache. 4ever.

TRAVELER'S CHECKS

Signed (and then countersigned) pre-debit-card paper currency, often used by Americans abroad; could be refunded if lost or stolen or forged; married the accountability of credit cards with the inflexibility of using cash and the extra paperwork of writing checks.

TUBE SETS

Big monitors that spent lifetimes taking up most of the room on your desk and/or in your living room, but never offered to do the dishes.

• • •

For half a century, you set up your living room with one thing in mind: Where is the TV going to go? During those years, the device in question was most likely a set made with cathode ray tubes—a.k.a., a CRT or tube TV. These monsters had presence: width, depth, and heft. In addition to being big, they were funnel-shaped. At their backs, they had a cathode—a kind of electron gun—which fired multicolored electrons toward the front via a vacuum tube. Magnets at the neck of the funnel determined the direction of the rays, which would make their image by going through a fine mesh (this created pixels), and then lighting up the phosphorous coating on the inside of the curved glass screen. The technology changed very little after its invention in the late 1890s. The bigger the screen, the bigger the tube had to be—and the more your household started to seem like it revolved around a washing machine that had one side which occasionally showed images of Peter Jennings or the Drummond family.

For the first few decades following the birth of the CRT screen, televisions were often sold pre-installed in cabinets, but eventually most sets required that you purchase your own deep shelving, which was described with the hopeful term "entertainment center." No, it usually wasn't a pretty thing, but at least it was a place to put the hulking TV . . . and the TiVo, and the DVD player, VCR, stereo system, Xbox,

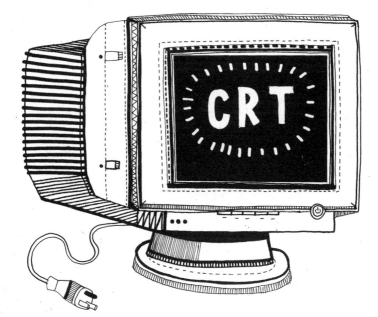

and PlayStation—all the trappings required to show that you'd arrived in society. Or at least into the lower middle-class. Yes, the tube television took up a lot of room, but you were willing to make that sacrifice. It cost enough to warrant a place of honor.

CRTs were also in our offices. In the 1970s, they were sometimes synonymous with computers—and therefore discussed with a kind of apprehensive reverence. "CRTs glow eerily at [the United Press International] headquarters in New York and at ten AP regional 'hubs' across the US," reported a *Time* magazine article in 1973. "When stories began vanishing into electronic limbo, the [*Detroit*] *News* was forced to modify its CRTs so that the 'kill' button must be hit twice before a story dies."

That's right: CRT screens could kill! Actually, they *could*: A falling CRT did in a nurse who was treating victims of the Oklahoma City bombings in 1995. But those were hardly the first tears that a tube TV or monitor had caused. For one thing, they were really heavy. For another, they often made a kind of high-pitched noise. Some people couldn't hear it, but if you did it was hard to tune out. Their fluorescent glare was known to cause headaches. They also had the habit of sometimes displaying ghost images, called "burn-ins": If any one part of the glass' internal phosphorous coating was stimulated for too long, it'd give off a faint glow—even when the screen wasn't on (you could see it a lot on arcade game displays if there was an element on screen that rarely moved). One attempt to combat this "burn-in" effect was the creation of screen savers: The flying toasters or ersatz digital fish tanks or dots being sucked into a vortex ensured that no one image ever stayed on the screen for any amount of time.

Mostly, however, tube TVs were awfully sturdy behemoths that could go decades without being replaced, and were lugged from one walk-up apartment to the next (that's what friends were for). And their computer cousins were equally reliable, and even provided a nice flat surface on which to display that bobblehead collection.

Liquid crystal display screens, known as LCDs, use light and heat to affect liquid crystals that determine the color of every pixel and don't need any tubes—ergo, no bulky backs. They aren't perfect, in that images can be hard to see from certain angles and often aren't as crisp as on tube screens. There's also the fact that you sometimes plug in a new set and find that a pixel has already died, leaving a black dot in its wake. On the upside, however, LCD sets save energy and reduce eye strain. They also look cool. When they began showing up in stores in the 90s, people took notice. With their big screens and small footprint, they seemed to offer a happy solution for families who wanted a television but didn't want to sacrifice a quarter of their living room. Indeed, a household's aesthete was just as likely to lobby for one as the resident couch potato. These TVs could sit on shallow shelves or even hang on walls. In the mid-aughts, their prices came down considerably. They accounted for less than 5 percent of all media screens in 2002, but in 2005 Sony announced that it was pulling the plug on production of thirty-four- and thirty-six-inch tube sets made at its Pittsburgh facility and would close its sprawling San Diego facility. By 2007, LCD screens were outselling CRTs. By 2009, they accounted for more than 95 percent of all televisions and computer monitors on the market.

The only problem is that desks can seem uncomfortably roomy without a big old CRT. Most desks aren't designed for skinny screens— they're usually so deep that if you put the LCD monitor by the wall, it's too far away. Some people solve the problem by mounting their monitors to adjustable arms attached to the wall or the desk, but the mounts are often as expensive as the screens. Most people have just accepted that there's going to be a whole lot of wasted desk real estate in the dead zone between the monitor and the wall. LCD TVs, meanwhile, are stealing space from walls that were once home to Matisse posters and canvases from "starving artists" sales. The farther the monitor is from the couch, the bigger the screen needs to be, and the more inclined people are to spend a disproportionate amount of their salary on something showing programming that they could just as easily get on their laptops.

Some, however, are still using their CRT monitors and tube TVs, if only because they don't have the closet space to store them in: Many Salvation Army and Goodwill centers now refuse to accept anything but flat screens.

TYPEWRITERS

Invaluable devices for creating neatly spaced blather.

• • •

Once, not so long ago, a tortured writer could easily spend days coming up with the perfect first sentence. It started out in the far reaches of the brain and made its way to the hands, which told the fingers exactly what keys to press in order to perform the little sonata that would result in letters inked on a page. Then the whole thing would end up in the wastebasket. Why fail alone when you can bring a couple trees down with you?

There was a soundtrack to the process—the creak of the paper roller, the satisfying click that sounded with each keystroke, and the celebratory bell that rang at the end of each sentence to indicate it was time to place a hyphen in that word and press return (on an electric machine) or manually shift the carriage. Your typing style depended on the kind of document you were producing: Something that was personal might be filled with words crossed out using rows of Xs; a formal letter would mean you'd want to carefully apply correction fluid (see page 48); a manuscript would require sandwiching carbon paper between two crisp white sheets so that you'd have a copy for editing or safe keeping.

Typewriters revolutionized the writing process just as drastically as computers did later. Today, drafts usually aren't saved at all (although they may be reclaimed, at least in part, with some massaging of the "Undo" command) and many letters, manuscripts, and school assignments will never exist on a physical piece of paper. Writing and editing so often happen concurrently; we shift around paragraphs and strike out sentences that may have been perfectly fine where they were if only they'd had a chance to settle in.

On the typewriter, it was common to complete an entire draft before revising a document. But people weren't always so fastidious. Sometimes the laborious nature of the process and the permanency of the medium simply meant that a writer had to lower his standards. In order to save paper or ink or sanity, many had a first-draft rule: Once you had something on paper, it was locked there for good and you were just going to have to live with it. There was no temptation to delete or fuss with fonts. It was a method that forced you to actually think before you typed—which is hard to imagine in this logorrheic era of blogs about comments written on blogs about blogs.

The first typewriters date back to the early nineteenth century. As telegraph machines became prevalent and offices began employing stenographers, an increasing number of office workers could speedily write and read shorthand and Morse code but could only transcribe as quickly as they could write longhand. Handwriting, done with a quill and ink at the time, was slow and often hard to read; it was clear there was desperate need for a fast way to produce printed words, and this motivated many an inventor.

William Austin Burt's 1829 "typographer" was the earliest attempt. It was a wooden box that had the type mounted on a semicircular frame that was inked using pads. The user moved the wheel by hand until it stopped at the desired letter. Charles Thurber introduced the idea of a cylindrical roller to hold the paper with his "printing machine" in 1843. Several inventors made models that looked almost identical to pianos. Many early ones could not produce punctuation or lowercase letters or numbers (a few models had keys for 2 through 9, with the typist instructed to use the letters O and I for zero and one).

In the 1860s Christopher Latham, a Wisconsin newspaperman, came up with the most useable typewriter model, which had a carriage

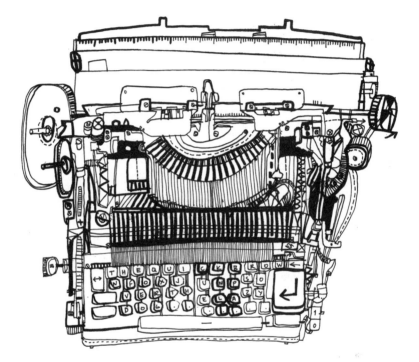

for the paper and rows of keys attached to individual moving metal bars. It looked a lot like the typewriters that were used throughout the twentieth century, except that the actual printing happened within the machine and therefore couldn't be seen until an entire page was complete. The keys were in the QWERTY layout that we still use: Although there are various guesses as to why the letters were laid out non-alphabetically, the prevailing theory is that they were placed unusually in order to keep people from typing so fast that the machine would jam. (It's also possible that it was a layout designed especially for store salesmen—they'd need only memorize the letters of the top row in order to show off how quickly one could type the word "typewriter.")

The Remington company produced the first models of Mr. Sholes's invention in 1874. The first typed book manuscript was *The Adventures of Tom Sawyer*, which Mark Twain delivered to his publishers in 1876. He also wrote testimonials for Remington. "Please do not divulge the fact that I own a machine," he wrote for one of the ad catalogs in 1875. "I have entirely stopped using the Type-Writer, for the reason that I never could write a letter with it to anybody without receiving a request by return mail that I would not only describe the machine but state what progress I had made in the use of it, etc., etc. I don't like to write letters, and so I don't want people to know that I own this curiosity breeding little joker."

Typewriters transformed businesses in many ways. Most notably, they brought women into the workplace. There are multiple theories about why typing was, early on, thought to be women's work. Part of it may have been due to the influence of the Remington company, which decorated its typewriters with flowers and gave them foot pedals in order to make them resemble the company's other major product: sewing machines. It also didn't hurt sales when typewriter companies encouraged business owners to believe that they'd *have to* hire pretty young women if they bought one of the newfangled machines. Whatever the reason, the typing schools of the early twentieth century were pumping out a steady stream of young women who were ready to take their seats at dictation desks. There was even a momentary craze for typing competitions, with various typewriter manufacturers sending especially groomed typists-cum-athletes to type-offs around the country.

But by the time humming electric machines buzzed on desks in the mid-twentieth century people were no longer so fascinated by the contraptions. Typewriters swiftly became both as essential and interesting as air. Christopher Latham never had the same name recognition as Bill Gates or Steve Jobs. But maybe the machines' reliability was the cause of people's disinterest. "They are too good for people," wrote one repairman in a 1954 book about typewriters. "They last too long. They work too well. If they were a lot more trouble than they are, typists would be more interested in them."

Although typewriters are still common in some developing nations, few American writers can be found toiling on them in the twenty-first century. Robert Caro, author of *The Power Broker*, uses one, as does film critic Andrew Sarris. The writer Paul Auster has been using his white manual Olympia typewriter for more than thirty years. "It's battered and obsolete—a relic from an age that is quickly passing from memory," he wrote in an ode to the humble machine in 2000, "but the damn thing has never given out on me." It's awfully hard to make the same claim about a laptop.

UNDERSCORES/UNDERLINES

Used in print for emphasis or to delineate that something is a title; necessary before upscale typewriters, word processors, and computers made it possible to use italic type, which makes important things look like they are being blown to the right side of the page.

UNFLATTERING MATERNITY CLOTHES

Roomy garments, often with Peter Pan collars, designed to provide comfort and show modesty—hey, everyone already knows you like to do it.

VACUUM TUBES

Bulb-like devices that created electric signals by controlling electrons within low-pressure confines; used in old radios, TVs, and in early computers—but not in actual household vacuums.

VIDEOS

Book-sized black plastic rectangles that allowed people to record television programs and gave cinephiles the ability to build comprehensive film libraries without investing in a projector or wasting a bedsheet.

• • •

In the late 1960s, Richard Diehl, a twelve-year-old technology buff, read an article about an invention that seemed unbelievable. "It said there were these recorders that would allow you to record what was on TV, and that was an idea that just blew my mind. What a concept," says Mr. Diehl. Ten years later, he put down two months' salary in order to purchase a black-and-white video recorder and a $70 tape that had to be manually fed through the open-reel machine.

"I loved lacing the tape by hand—winding it up and setting the tension and feeling it with my fingers," he says. Early video recorders took a certain artistry to operate, and Mr. Diehl, who'd grow up to be one of Southern California's most respected VCR repairmen, considered himself a virtuoso. "I'd listen to the motors whirling and I developed an ear to be able to tell when something wasn't right. There was kind of a priesthood syndrome—like, 'I'm in charge of this powerful thing and you don't know anything about it.'"

Not knowing quite how to use your video cassette recorder was, for many years, shorthand for feeling confused by modern technology and ill-equipped to deal with a mysterious device that could enable you to both attend night school and keep up on J.R.'s latest escapades on *Dallas*. Early video devotees were indeed a little drunk on the power of being able to watch TV on their own terms, sometimes even chauffeuring their gargantuan machines to cities where their desired show would be airing so they could capture it on tape, or to hotels that offered closed circuit movies so that they could capture an at-home copy of their favorite film. Each week, Hugh Hefner famously took his *TV Guide*, highlighted every show and movie he wanted to see, and then passed on the list to a secretary who had been hired specifically to operate the machine and then catalog tapes for him in his growing library. When Sony's Betamax and JVC's VHS pre-threaded cassettes hit the market at affordable prices in 1975, anyone could do this kind of "time shifting" (if only they could figure out how to program the darn thing). Sony advertised their Betamax tapes with the tagline: "You don't have to miss *Kojak* because you're watching *Columbo*." It was a moment where it seemed there could finally be peace on Earth.

"I remember in 1978 giving a friend a $30 blank tape to record *Dark Star* from Showtime for me," Mr. Diehl says, wistfully. "I still have that tape."

It took a while for movie studios to catch on to the idea that they might actually be able to profit from offering their movies on tape. Originally, the machines were advertised exclusively as devices that could record TV for later viewing, not as machines that could show prerecorded content. Blank tapes were more of a commodity than prerecorded ones. But by the late 80s, studios were making more from selling tapes of recent films than they were making in the theaters.

Playing a tape was unlike any previous movie-watching experience, because of the fact that you had to physically interact with the medium—whether that meant running to the machine to stop recording during commercials or pasting together broken tape or trying to find a blank cassette before erasing *On the Waterfront* so you could record *The Great Muppet Caper*. When only one tape was around, sometimes such sacrifices had to be made.)

The explosion of movies on video spawned a generation of movie lovers who were able to absorb films from any decade or any country without having to wait for something to be revived at the local art house theater. It also made for more informed viewers. Brian De Palma's 1976 film *Obsession* was nearly identical in plot to Alfred Hitchcock's *Vertigo*, but he nevertheless released it with impunity, gambling that not many of *Obsession*'s viewers would have seen *Vertigo*, which had been released two decades earlier. Seeing an old movie would've meant getting copies of the reels of film and then projecting them yourself. "Before video, it was a lot easier to knock things off because no one else had seen them," notes director Paul Schrader.

There was much argument regarding which format was better. If you bought a Betamax player, you weren't going to be able to play tapes made for a VHS, and vice versa. By the mid 80s, VHS tapes cornered the market for at-home video watchers and recorders, despite the fact that Betamax cassettes, which hit shelves the same year, actually were believed to make superior recordings. In the interim, there was an ongoing debate regarding which was the best system to buy. Eventually, people shirked quality for quantity: VHS could tape things that were considerably longer. But in the late 90s, DVDs began to pose a threat. In 2003, annual DVD rentals started to outnumber video rentals. Today, TiVo and DVR boxes have made "time shifting" a luxury that's so commonplace it's easy to take it for granted.

Mr. Diehl, who has a collection of over 160 types of video recorders, still occasionally gets calls from people trying to figure out how to restore an old tape or thread a long-discontinued machine. He doesn't deny that DVDs and digital television offer a level of clarity and ease that video never could reach, but he can't help but miss the power that the video-expert wielded, and the comparatively simple technology behind video tapes. "When something is no longer mechanical, it becomes cold and commonplace and taken for granted," he says. "I could explain videos to anyone who has a basic knowledge of circuits. But your average person out there—he's just never going to really get how digital things work."

VIDEO STORES

Rental shops providing movies prerecorded onto tapes and curated at the whim of the shop's staff; required a membership fee that was good for your lifetime or the store's—whichever was shorter.

• • •

With the birth of video came an influx of stores that emitted a siren's call that was irresistible to those who were equal parts tech-nerd and cinephile; in the 1980s, these little rental libraries became salons for discussion of everything from the relative merits of Marx Brothers films to Bruce Lee's choreography (punctuated with excoriations of those who dared to not rewind). If you were a civilian walking into a video store, you could state your mood and your taste and you'd likely be met with a barrage of suggestions from a teenager who'd seen more films in a year than many adults had seen in their lives. Working at a video store was a dream job for anyone who fancied the idea of getting paid to sit indoors and stare at a TV while flipping through Leonard Maltin's latest movie guide and spewing half-baked critical theory.

Some video store clerks ruled their shops like little fiefdoms. Daniel Noah, a screenwriter who started working at the now-shuttered Kim's Videos on Saint Mark's Place in New York City in 1992, recalls employees scaring away many customers who, say, dared to pronounce the last "d" in "Godard." They were just as likely to fawn over the handful of regulars who seemed to have a passable knowledge of film history; regulars like Martin Scorsese. "We were super-opinionated.

I think people were often intimidated to rent from us. If you asked to see the new releases section, for example, you'd be ridiculed," says Mr. Noah. "There were even people on staff who would criticize people's choice of porn." Staffers at Kim's didn't just ridicule their clients to their faces: There were plenty of regulars whose eclectic tastes provided fodder for conversation during off-hours. "We would analyze people by their movie rentals. Like, if someone looked cool but only got romantic comedies, we'd mock him a little. Or we'd try to analyze the psyche of someone who was really into Jim Jarmusch, but also kept getting chick flicks. And whenever a cute girl came in, we'd *instantly* go look at her rental record. If she liked foreign films, it was love."

Tapes were usually categorized by genre or era or country of origin, with alphabetization used only as an afterthought. It was the only place in a strip mall that was as popular with eight-year-olds as it was with adults looking for porn—and there were more than a few cases of people purposely switching tapes, leaving flummoxed old men doing their best to satisfy themselves while watching *Jem*.

When franchises like Blockbuster took over the market, they were cavernous affairs filled with countless shelves of empty video boxes, each of which represented little more than the idea of a movie that may or not have been in stock. They needed to be traded in at the counter in order to get the actual tape. Still, conditioned as you were to shopping for tomatoes or Ziploc bags by cruising down aisles of tangible goods, you never questioned shopping in this way for a piece of media that could've just as easily been housed in a card catalog.

Most of the clerks were in charge of collecting the membership fees that were levied in order to help the owners build their stock—movie studios charged stores as much as $100 per cassette. Usually, the membership rigmarole was rather informal, but larger stores often asked for everything short of a urine sample. And you gladly gave it. Then you went home and were warned that the FBI would jail you for life if you dared to copy the thing. These video people didn't play around.

VISIBLE ORTHODONTURE

Pre-Invisalign bulky metal dental apparatuses designed to correct tooth alignment and to ensure that a child would receive the requisite amount of character-building peer mockery.

WHITE PAGES

Phone directories which were distributed for free, but took up infinitely more shelf space than online directories; the thick books no longer seemed comprehensive once people began relying on cell phone numbers, which were not listed. Even Edward Saxon, a film producer who made a hobby of creating aliases that would be listed either first or last in the *Manhattan White Pages*, has stopped letting his fingers do the walking. He retired both Aaron A-aabba and Zelmo Zzzzzip when he moved to Los Angeles in 2005. "I still get them delivered to my door," says Mr. Saxon. "But they get recycled right away."

WRINKLES

Skin creases and lines formerly considered the natural physical result of either old age or sleeping on crumpled sheets.

• • •

How can you tell if someone is old? Is it a calculation that involves the number of teeth on the bridge soaking in an old mayonnaise jar by the side of the bed at night? Perhaps you need to multiply that by the hours per week that Charlie Rose is your main source of company? Why don't we just pick a number. How about seventy? That is, unless *you* happen to be seventy . . .

"Old" used to be a word that was easily defined. No one would've gasped to hear it thrown about in reference to the wizened, wrinkled grandma in the yellowing photo on the mantle. Hadn't she matured to a state where vanity and folly were interchangeable terms? If she didn't look like she had another fifty years ahead of her, that was probably because she didn't. She wasn't interested in false advertising.

For millennia, however, there's been a subset of people who've developed permanent furrows in their brows while trying to battle the aging process. It's a club that has seen its membership balloon in recent years, thanks to the fact that the population of people living beyond middle age has never been so sizable: There are currently close to forty million people aged sixty-five or over in the United States, with their ranks growing at twice the rate of any other age group. It's largely for their sakes that doctors have concocted synthetic "filler" injections to make cheeks and mouth corners plump where they once may have been sunken in. Surgeons can use their scalpels and threads to hike up saggy foreheads with little more effort than yanking up a knee sock. Botox injections will paralyze muscles that have created deep facial creases, etched by years of use.

These procedures aren't just appealing to an older set. In addition to loading up on SPF-filled unguents and shelling out cash for micro-dermabrasion treatments that promise to make even young skin look younger, there are frequently people under thirty in dermatologists' offices lining up for Botox injections. Their hope is that by paralyzing their brows and upper lips now, those muscles won't get used enough to cause wrinkle lines at a later date.

Indeed, modern man doesn't age gracefully. He prefers not to age at all.

"I have patients who get regular Botox shots in the same way that you or I might get our teeth cleaned or get a trim," says one Los Angeles dermatologist who injects his patients with dozens of shots of this FDA-approved form of the botulinum toxin every day. "It's considered 'maintenance' to them. They know that they'll never look like teenagers again, but they want to show that they're making an effort. It's not unlike how gray-haired society women used to put blue rinse in their hair. The point wasn't that it looked natural—they just felt it added a richness to their hair. It was something they could do to make themselves look more put together. It was a way for them to show that they were still with it enough to put in the effort. That in and of itself can make someone seem more youthful than they would otherwise."

Unfortunately, modern anti-wrinkle treatments can leave people looking more odd than old. Some surgeries and shots have been known to create facial angles that are a little too harsh, and expressions that are sort of . . . well, it'd be generous to call them expressions at all. Youth, which once gave way to soft lines and saggy skin, liver spots and sunken areas, is now just as likely to mature into something sharp and excessively taut. People don't grow older as much as they grow tighter.

It's worth remembering that there are many societies out there that revere their elders—at least that's what our society's elders would probably want us to believe, if we actually had anyone around there who copped to being elderly. Yes, we do sometimes wax on about how growing old is as blessed a process as aging wine . . . but we only say this when the person growing old is someone else. Wrinkles, like rings on a tree, are a testament to the years of wisdom one has required, right? Each laugh line and crow's-foot is a symbol of a life well lived; those permanently pruned fingers a joyous reminder of those happy years of washing dishes—oh, what fun we had! Shar-pei–like bags under one's eyes and sagging upper arms are proof that you worked hard, played hard, and were so devil-may-care that you left the Coppertone at home.

The problem with this seemingly generous parlance is that it suggests that today, by the look of the unmarred swaths of skin found on the faces of the most "mature" people among us, no one is having much fun at all.

WRISTWATCHES

Miniature clocks worn on the wrist and checked periodically; until battery-operated ones were made in the mid-1900s, they had to be wound regularly. Supplanted pocket watches, which, as Jonathan Swift suggested in *Gulliver's Travels*, were as important to man as God. They eventually included calculators and alarm clocks, with many people postulating that the future would be full of people using wrist-bound devices such as video phones. Still worn as jewelry, but less commonly purchased for utility: Instead we get our time from (and worship) pocket-dwelling cell phones.

WRITING LETTERS

Method of communication usually involving paper, pen, and the US Postal Service; basic structure included a salutation (e.g., "Dear John" or "Hi Mom"), body ("It's over" or "Camp is good"), signature ("Sincerely, Jean" or "Love, Me"), and optional postscript ("P.S. You'll be hearing from my lawyer" or "Please send a bra").

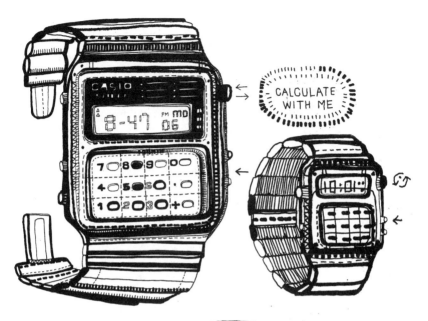

CALCULATE WITH ME

ACKNOWLEDGMENTS

I'd like to thank a few of the people in my life who didn't say: "Oh, your book is called *Obsolete*? Does that mean you're writing about me?" James Horowitz, Melissa Antonelli, Shazia Ahmad, Melanie Friedson, Jessica Kramer, and my parents, Vicki Morgan and Robert Grossman, were kind enough to read drafts and help me brainstorm many, many of the ideas that lie herein. I'm also grateful to Sandy Fernández and Tom Shroder of the *Washington Post Magazine* for assigning me the article that led to this book. It'd be nearly impossible to acknowledge everyone who gave me feedback and suggested definitions that made their way into these pages, but among the people who really devoted needless amounts of energy to helping me are Ralph Erenzo, Ruth Graham, Jessica Vitkus, Ed Herro, Max Frey, Daisy Carrington, Ronda Kaysen, Jonathan Bender, Emma Rathbone, Susannah Lescher, Carole Borstein, Yaniv Soha, Ian Blecher, Bobbie Rothman, Julie Hoffman, and Emma Fensterheim. Finally, I'd like to thank the two Davids— Halpern, my agent, and Cashion, my editor—for giving me the opportunity to do this, and making the whole process a lot of fun.

SELECTED BIBLIOGRAPHY

Agoglia, Justin. "How Hotel Keys Taught Me a Lesson About Honesty,"
<http://www.joeagoglia.com/stories/keys.asp>

Alterman, Eric. "Out of Print." *The New Yorker*. 31 Mar 2008. 12 Feb 2009.
<http://newyorker.com/reporting/2008/03/31/080331fa_fact_alterman>

Auster, Paul and Sam Messer. *The Story of My Typewriter*. New York:
Distributed Art Publishers, Inc., 2002.

Baldwin, Kevin. *Bald*. New York: Bloomsbury, 2005.

Barber, Charles. *Comfortably Numb: How Psychiatry Is Medicating a Nation*.
New York: Pantheon Books, 2008.

Baue, William. "Phase-out of Mercury Thermometers Continues to Rise."
Sustainability Investment News. 10 Jan 2002. 31 Jan 2009. <http://www.
socialfunds.com/news/article.cgi/752.html>

Biskind, Peter. *Easy Riders, Raging Bulls: How the Sex-Drugs-and-Rock 'N' Roll
Generation Saved Hollywood*. New York: Touchstone/Simon & Schuster, 1998.

Bliven, Jr., Bruce. *The Wonderful Writing Machine*. New York: Random
House, 1954.

Brenton, Sam, and Reuben Cohen. *Shooting People: Adventures in Reality TV*.
London: Verso, 2003.

Brenton, Myron. The Privacy Invaders. New York: Crest Books, 1964.

Brown, AmyJo. "No Diving?" *Pool & Spa News*. Jan 2004: 1.

Brownfield, Paul. "Serious Issue of Canned Laughter." *Los Angeles Times*. 4
Sept 1998: F1.

Brunvand, Jan. *The Truth Never Stands in the Way of a Good Story*. Chicago:
University of Illinois Press, 2001.

Cobb, Nathan. "Rolodex Cards: A Triumph of Low Technology." *Boston
Globe*. 17 Nov 1988: 81.

Cranz, Galen. *The Chair*. New York: W. W. Norton & Company, 2000.

Crystal, David. *Txting: The Gr8 Db8*. *Oxford*: New York: Oxford University
Press, 2008.

Cullen, Lisa Takeuchi, and Tracy Schmidt. "Today's Nun Has a Veil—And
a Blog." *Time*. 13 Nov 2006. 13 Feb 2009. <http://www.time.com/time/
magazine/article/0,9171,1558292,00.html>

Dahlberg, Edwin. *I Pick Up Hitchhikers*. Valley Forge: Judson Press, 1978.

Del Conte, Natali. "Survey: Teens Use E-Mail Less Than Anyone
Else." *PC*. 6 Nov 2006. 10 Feb 2009. <http://www.foxnews.com/
story/0,2933,227721,00.html>

Davis, Susan. "After the Beep . . ." *San Francisco Examiner*. 11 Feb 1990:

D19–D20.

Douglas, Susan J. *Listening In: Radio and the American Imagination*. New York: Times Books/Random House, 1999.

Ehrenfeld, David. *Beginning Again*. New York: Oxford University Press, 1993.

Fischer, Claudes. *America Calling: A Social History of the Telephone to 1940*. Berkeley: University of California Press, 1992.

Florey, Kitty Burns. *Script & Scribble: The Rise and Fall of Handwriting*. Brooklyn: Melville House Publishing, 2009.

Fogg, B. J., and Daisuke Iizawa. "Online Persuasion in Facebook and Mixi: A Cross-Cultural Comparison." *Persuasive Technology*. Oulu, Finland: Springer, 2008. 35–46.

Friess, Steve. "A Gift Can Leave You in Stitches." *USA Today*. 21 Dec 2006: 9D.

Gladwell, Malcolm. *Blink*. New York: Little, Brown and Company, 2005.

Greenberg, Joshua M. *From Betamax to Blockbuster*. Cambridge, MA: The MIT Press, 2008.

Hall, Trish. "With Phones Everywhere, Everyone Is Talking More." *New York Times*. 11 Oct 1989: 1.

Hanlon, Evan. "Love It, Hate It: Text Messaging." *Harvard Crimson*. 4 Oct. 2004. 30 Oct 2008. <http://thecrimson.com/article.aspx?ref=503805>

Hirschorn, Michael. "End Times." *Atlantic Monthly*. Jan/Feb 2009. 9 Feb 2009. <http://www.theatlantic.com/doc/200901/new-york-times>

Jonas, Susan, and Marilyn Nissenson. *Going, Going, Gone: Vanishing Americana*. San Francisco: Chronicle Books, 1994.

Keller, Bill. "Not Dead Yet: The Newspaper in the Days of Digital Anarchy." *The Guardian*. 29 Nov 2007. 12 Feb 2009. <http://guardian.co.uk/media/2007/nov/29/pressandpublishing.digitalmedia1>

Lehman, Charles. *Handwriting Models for Schools*. Portland: The Alcuin Press, 1976.

McAdam, E. L., and George Milne, eds. *Johnson's Dictionary: A Modern Selection*. Mineola: Dover Publications, 2005.

McKee W.J. "A Controlled Study of the Effects of Tonsillectomy and Adenoidectomy in Children." *British Journal of Preventive & Social Medicine* (17). April 1963: 49–69.

Meyer, Philip. *The Vanishing Newspaper*. Columbia: University of Missouri Press, 2004.

Morales, Lymari. "Cable, Internet News Sources Growing in Popularity." Gallup. 15 Dec 2008. 13 Feb 2009. <http://www.gallup.com/poll/113314/Cable-Internet-News-Sources-Growing-Popularity.aspx>

Murph, Darren. "Worldwide LCD TV Shipments Surpass CRTs for First Time Ever." EndgadetHD. 19 Feb 2008. 14 Feb 2009. <http://www.engadgethd.com/2008/02/19/worldwide-lcd-tv-shipments-surpass-crts-for-first-time-ever/>

"News by Computer." *Time.* 17 Dec 1973. 13 Feb 2009. <http://www.time.com/time/magazine/article/0,9171,908337,00.html>

Picken, Mary Brooks. *Mending Made Easy.* New York: Harper & Brothers, 1943.

Nunberg, Geoffrey, ed. *The Future of the Book.* Berkeley: University of California Press, 1996.

Paul, Pamela. *Pornified.* New York: Times Books/Henry Holt and Company, 2005.

Phaidon Design Classics. London: Phaidon Press Limited, 2006.

Post, Peggy. *Emily Post's Etiquette (17th Edition).* New York: HarperResource, 2004.

Reardon, Marguerite. "Americans Text More Than They Talk." *CNET News.* 22 Sept 2008. 10 Feb 2009. <http://news.cnet.com/8301-1035_3-10048257-94.html>

Roberts, Kenneth. *It Must Be Your Tonsils.* Garden City: Doubleday, Doran & Co., 1936.

Rosman, Katherine. "Clinging to the Rolodex." *Wall Street Journal.* 24 Nov 2007: W1.

Schuman, Michael. "Lean Machines." *Time.* 15 Dec 2002. 13 Feb 2009. <http://www.time.com/time/magazine/article/0,9171,400038,00.html>

Schweber, Bill. "My AM Radio's New Life." *Electronic Engineering Times.* 30 June 2008: 31.

Taub, Eric A. "Picture Tubes Are Fading Into the Past." *New York Times.* 7 Aug 2006. 13 Feb 2009 <http://nytimes.com/2006/08/07/technology/07tube.html>

"Telecom Milestone: More Cell-Phone Only Than Land-Only Households." Mediamark Research Inc., Press Release: 12 Sept 2007.

Toffler, Alvin. *Future Shock.* New York: Bantam Books, 1971.

Tuleja, Tad. *Curious Customs.* New York: Harmony Books, 1987.

Voltolina, Vanessa. "The Unlucky 47." *Folio.* 9 Feb 2009. 12 Feb 2009. <http://www.foliomag.com/2009/complete-47-09>

Weatherall, Ann. *Gender Language and Discourse.* East Sussex: Routledge, 2002.

Wyatt, Edward. "Electronic Device Stirs Unease at Book Fair." *New York Times.* 2 June 2008: E1.